At Sylvan, we believe that a lifelong love of learning begins at an early age, and we are glad you have chosen our resources to help your children experience the joy of mathematics as they build critical reasoning skills. We know that the time you spend with your children reinforcing the lessons learned in school will contribute to their love of learning.

Success in math requires more than just memorizing basic facts and algorithms; it also requires children to make sense of size, shape, and numbers as they appear in the world. Children who can connect their understanding of math to the world around them will be ready for the challenges of mathematics as they advance to more complex topics.

We use a research-based, step-by-step process in teaching math at Sylvan that includes thought-provoking math problems and activities. As students increase their success as problem solvers, they become more confident. With increasing confidence, students build even more success. The design of the Sylvan workbooks will help you to help your children build the skills and confidence that will contribute to success in school.

Included with your purchase of this workbook is a coupon for a discount at a participating Sylvan center. We hope you will use this coupon to further your children's academic journeys. Let us partner with you to support the development of confident, well-prepared, independent learners.

The Sylvan Team

1st Grade
Math
Games & Puzzles

Published in the United States by Random House, Inc., New York, and in Canada by Random House of Canada Limited, Toronto.

www.tutoring.sylvanlearning.com

Created by Smarterville Productions LLC
Producer & Editorial Direction: The Linguistic Edge
Producer: TJ Trochlil McGreevy
Writer: Amy Kraft
Cover and Interior Illustrations: Tim Goldman and Duendes del Sur
Layout and Art Direction: SunDried Penguin
Director of Product Development: Russell Ginns

First Edition

ISBN: 978-0-375-43035-0

This book is available at special discounts for bulk purchases for sales promotions or premiums. For more information, write to Special Markets/Premium Sales, 1745 Broadway, MD 6-2, New York, New York 10019 or e-mail specialmarkets@randomhouse.com.

PRINTED IN CHINA

10 9 8 7 6 5 4 3 2 1

Contents

Connect the Dots

DRAW a line to connect the numbers in order, starting with 1.

Criss Cross

WRITE each number word with one letter in each square.

Across →

3.

4.

5.

7.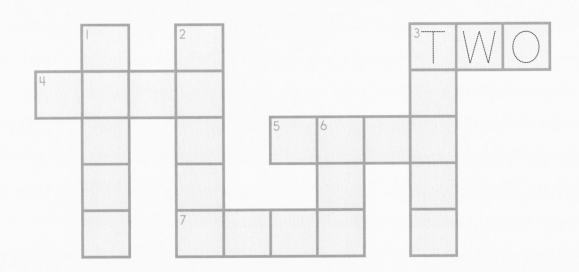

Down ↓

1.

2.

3.

6.

3. T W O

Domino Dots

Using the dominoes from pages 109 and 111, PLACE one domino in each blue space. Then ADD the number of dots on the top of the domino with the number of dots on the bottom, and WRITE the sum. (Save the dominoes to use again later in the workbook.)

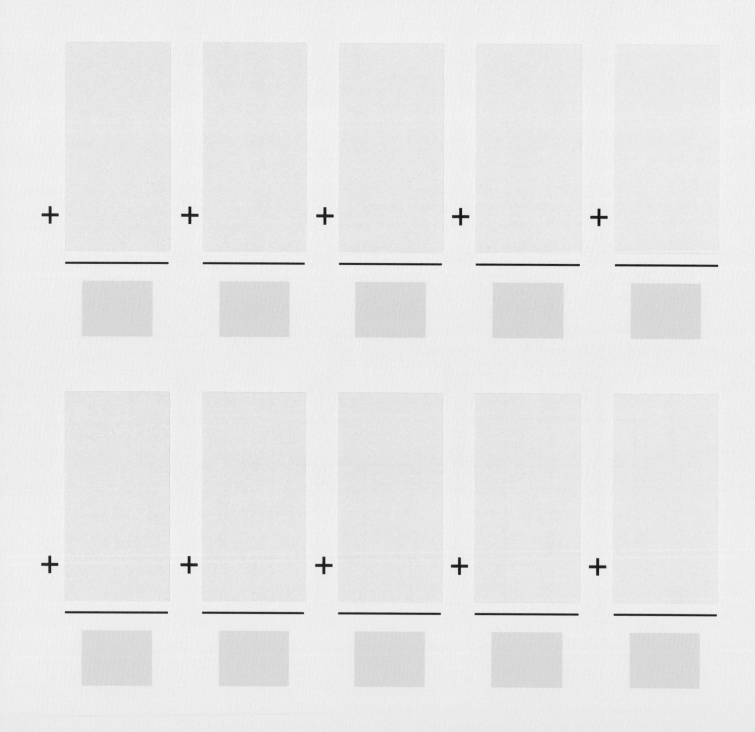

Safe Crackers

WRITE the sums. Then WRITE the sums from smallest to largest to find the right combination for the safe.

$$5 + 2 = \boxed{7}$$
1

$$3 + 3 = \boxed{}$$
2

$$1 + 4 = \boxed{}$$
3

$$1 + 1 = \boxed{}$$
4

$$6 + 3 = \boxed{}$$
5

$$8 + 0 = \boxed{}$$
6

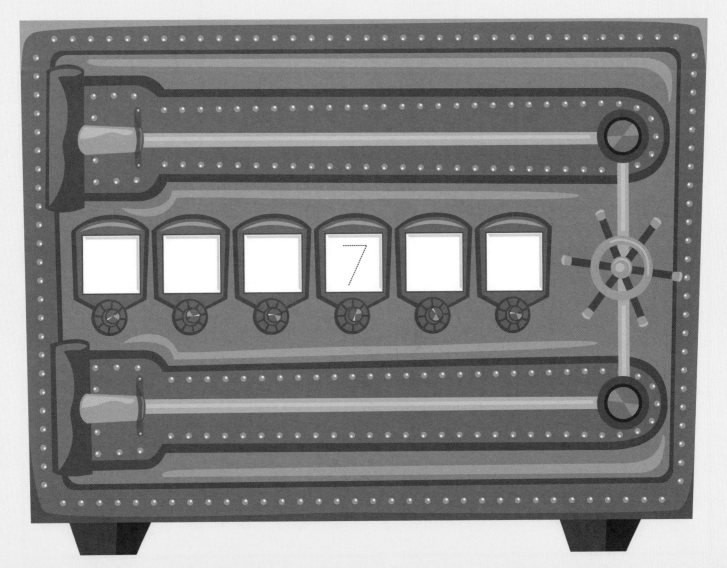

Mystery Number

WRITE the sums, and COLOR each section according to the numbers to reveal the mystery number.

8 =   10 =   5 =   4 =   7 =

$$7 + 1$$

$$5 + 2 =$$

$$1 + 3 =$$

$$9 + 1$$

$$5 + 0$$

$$4 + 1$$

$$4 + 6$$

$$2 + 2$$

$$2 + 6$$

$$1 + 6$$

$$4 + 3$$

$$2 + 3$$

$$4 + 4$$

$$3 + 2$$

$$4 + 0$$

$$8 + 2$$

$$4 + 0 =$$

$$0 + 7$$

$$7 + 3$$

$$2 + 2$$

$$10 + 0$$

$$0 + 5$$

$$8 + 0$$

$$3 + 5$$

$$1 + 4 =$$

$$5 + 5$$

$$1 + 3 =$$

Spin It

Use the spinner from page 113. SPIN the spinner once for each problem, and WRITE the number in the blue box. Then WRITE the sum in the red box. (Save the spinner to use again.)

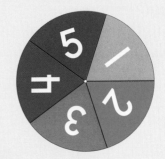

4 + ☐ = ☐

☐ + 1 = ☐

☐ + 2 = ☐

3 + ☐ = ☐

5 + ☐ = ☐

☐ + 4 = ☐

☐ + 3 = ☐

2 + ☐ = ☐

1 + ☐ = ☐

☐ + 5 = ☐

Your Deal

Using the number cards 2 through 7 from a deck of playing cards, DEAL a card onto each space. SAY the sum out loud. REPEAT until you have run out of cards.

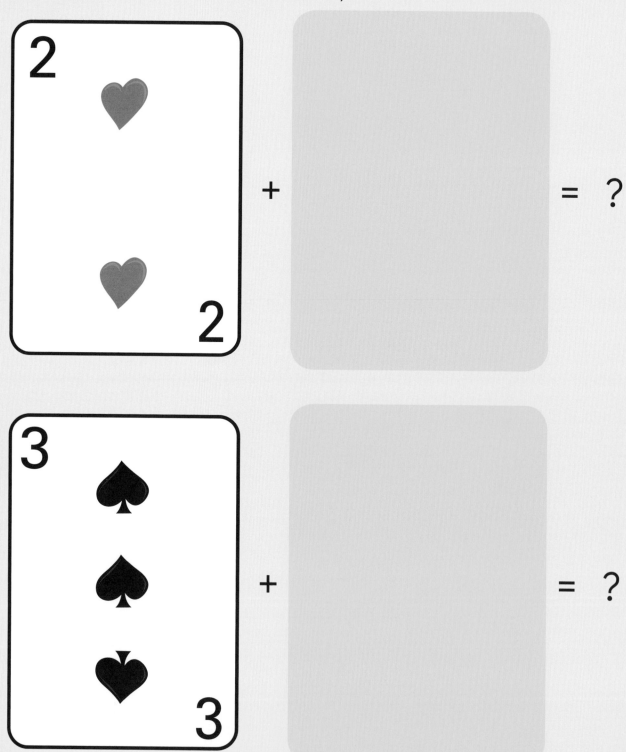

Code Breaker

SOLVE each problem. Then WRITE the letter or number that matches each sum to solve the riddle.

3 + 1 4 1 U	8 + 2 2 B	5 + 4 3 A	2 + 4 4 7	3 + 5 5 S	1 + 0 6 8
4 + 1 7 E	5 + 2 8 9	2 + 1 9 C			

Why is 6 afraid of 7?

U						
10	5	3	9	4	8	5

		!
6	1	7

Subtracting Differences from 10

Mystery Number

WRITE the differences, and COLOR each section according to the differences to reveal the mystery number.

1 =   2 =   3 =   4 =   5 =

$$\begin{array}{r} 9 \\ -4 \\ \hline \end{array}$$

$$\begin{array}{r} 8 \\ -6 \\ \hline \end{array}$$

$$7 - 4 =$$

$$\begin{array}{r} 1 \\ -0 \\ \hline \end{array}$$

$$10 - 9 =$$

$$\begin{array}{r} 6 \\ -2 \\ \hline \end{array}$$

$$\begin{array}{r} 5 \\ -4 \\ \hline \end{array}$$

$$9 - 5 =$$

$$\begin{array}{r} 7 \\ -3 \\ \hline \end{array}$$

$$\begin{array}{r} 9 \\ -7 \\ \hline \end{array}$$

$$\begin{array}{r} 3 \\ -1 \\ \hline \end{array}$$

$$\begin{array}{r} 4 \\ -0 \\ \hline \end{array}$$

$$\begin{array}{r} 5 \\ -3 \\ \hline \end{array}$$

$$10 - 8 =$$

$$8 - 5 =$$

$$\begin{array}{r} 5 \\ -1 \\ \hline \end{array}$$

$$\begin{array}{r} 10 \\ -6 \\ \hline \end{array}$$

$$\begin{array}{r} 5 \\ -2 \\ \hline \end{array}$$

$$\begin{array}{r} 4 \\ -0 \\ \hline \end{array}$$

$$\begin{array}{r} 7 \\ -2 \\ \hline \end{array}$$

$$\begin{array}{r} 7 \\ -3 \\ \hline \end{array}$$

$$\begin{array}{r} 6 \\ -5 \\ \hline \end{array}$$

$$\begin{array}{r} 10 \\ -6 \\ \hline \end{array}$$

$$\begin{array}{r} 2 \\ -0 \\ \hline \end{array}$$

$$\begin{array}{r} 5 \\ -1 \\ \hline \end{array}$$

$$\begin{array}{r} 8 \\ -7 \\ \hline \end{array}$$

$$\begin{array}{r} 6 \\ -2 \\ \hline \end{array}$$

$$\begin{array}{r} 4 \\ -3 \\ \hline \end{array}$$

$$\begin{array}{r} 6 \\ -4 \\ \hline \end{array}$$

$$\begin{array}{r} 5 \\ -0 \\ \hline \end{array}$$

$$10 - 7 =$$

Safe Crackers

WRITE the differences. Then WRITE the differences from largest to smallest to find the right combination for the safe.

$$10 - 8 =$$ $$5 - 1 =$$ $$6 - 3 =$$ $$9 - 1 =$$ $$8 - 2 =$$ $$7 - 7 =$$

1   2   3   4   5   6

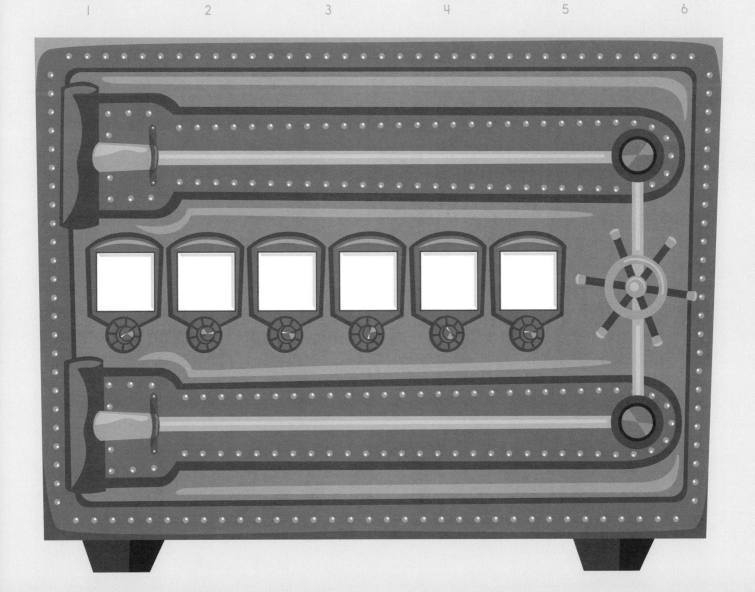

Subtracting Differences
from 10

Spin It

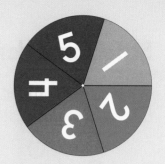

Use the spinner from page 113. SPIN the spinner once for each problem, and WRITE the number in the yellow box. Then WRITE the difference in the blue box. (Save the spinner to use again.)

10 − ☐ = ☐

7 − ☐ = ☐

8 − ☐ = ☐

5 − ☐ = ☐

6 − ☐ = ☐

9 − ☐ = ☐

7 − ☐ = ☐

10 − ☐ = ☐

5 − ☐ = ☐

8 − ☐ = ☐

Missing Middles

WRITE the number missing from the center square.

1.

```
      6
      -
9  -  [ ]  =  4
      =
      1
```

2.

```
      7
      -
1  -  [ ]  =  0
      =
      6
```

3.

```
      8
      -
10 -  [ ]  =  6
      =
      4
```

4.

```
      5
      -
7  -  [ ]  =  5
      =
      3
```

5.

```
      2
      -
4  -  [ ]  =  4
      =
      2
```

6.

```
      10
      -
8  -  [ ]  =  1
      =
      3
```

Subtracting Differences
from 10

Pipe Down

WRITE the missing number. Then FOLLOW the pipe, and WRITE the same number in the next problem.

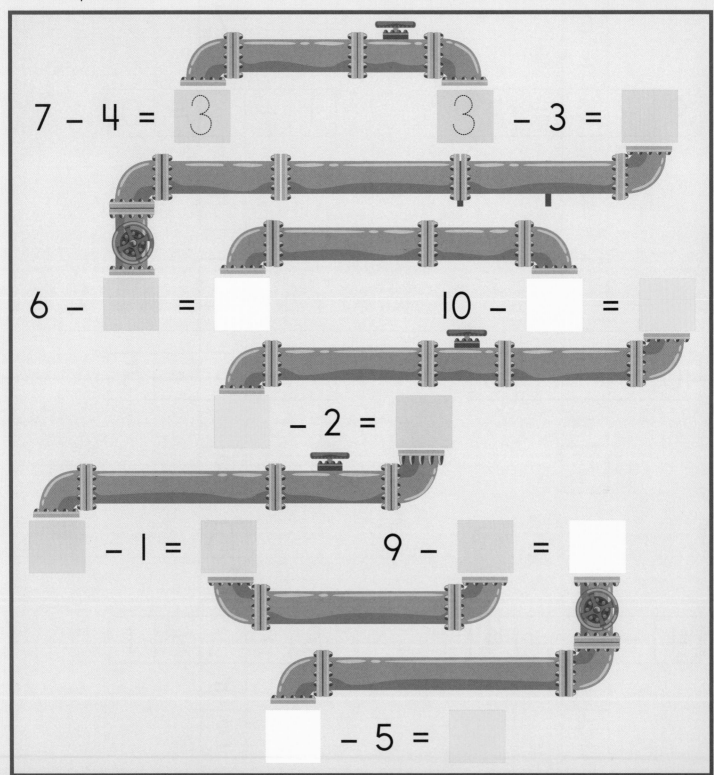

7 – 4 = 3   3 – 3 =

6 – ⬜ =   10 – ⬜ =

⬜ – 2 =

⬜ – 1 =   9 – ⬜ =

⬜ – 5 =

Space Walk

Using the numbers in the picture, WRITE as many fact families with the number 9 as you can.

HINT: A fact family shows all of the different ways that three numbers can be added and subtracted.

Example: 1 + 2 = 3
2 + 1 = 3
3 – 1 = 2
3 – 2 = 1

☐ + ☐ = ☐

☐ + ☐ = ☐

☐ – ☐ = ☐

☐ – ☐ = ☐

☐ + ☐ = ☐

☐ + ☐ = ☐

☐ – ☐ = ☐

☐ – ☐ = ☐

☐ + ☐ = ☐

☐ + ☐ = ☐

☐ – ☐ = ☐

☐ – ☐ = ☐

Super Sudoku

WRITE the numbers 1 through 4 so that each row, column, and box has all four numbers.

1	2	3	4
	4		2
2		4	
	3		1

	4	2	
1			3
2	3		4
		1	

WRITE the numbers 1 through 9 so that each row, column, and box has all nine numbers.

1		2		5	6	3	7	8
	3	4	9	2				
6		8	7		1	9		4
	2	1		6	9	7		5
		9			4		1	
8	7		5		2	6	4	9
	4		6		5		3	
3	8	6		4	7	5		2
9			2	8		4		7

Pipe Down

WRITE the missing number. Then FOLLOW the pipe, and WRITE the same number in the next problem.

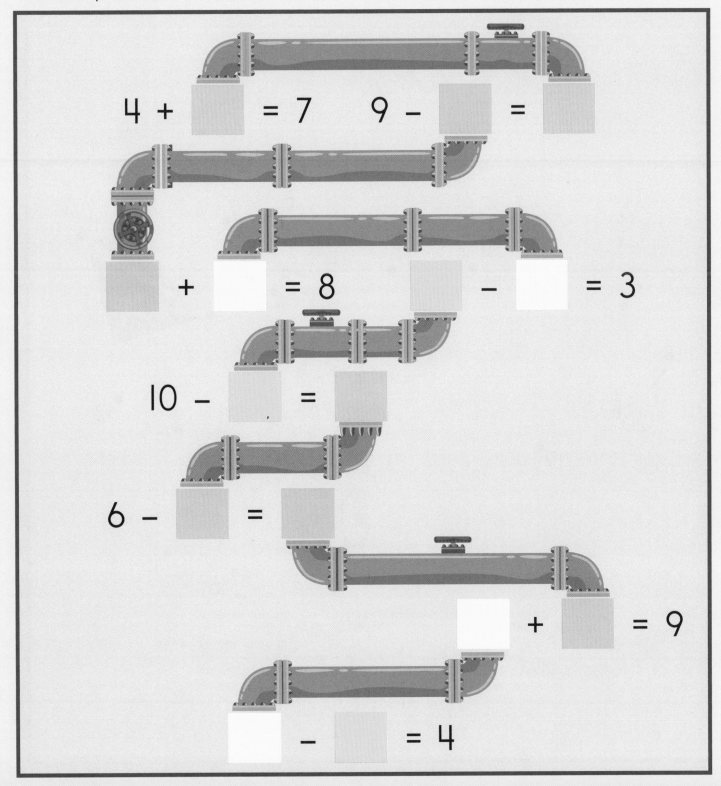

4 + ☐ = 7   9 − ☐ = ☐

☐ + ☐ = 8   ☐ − ☐ = 3

10 − ☐ = ☐

6 − ☐ = ☐

☐ + ☐ = 9

☐ − ☐ = 4

Connect the Dots

DRAW a line to connect the numbers in order, starting with 1.

Criss Cross

WRITE each number word with one letter in each square.

Across →

2. 15

3. 13

4. 12

5. 19

Down ↓

1. 20

2. 14

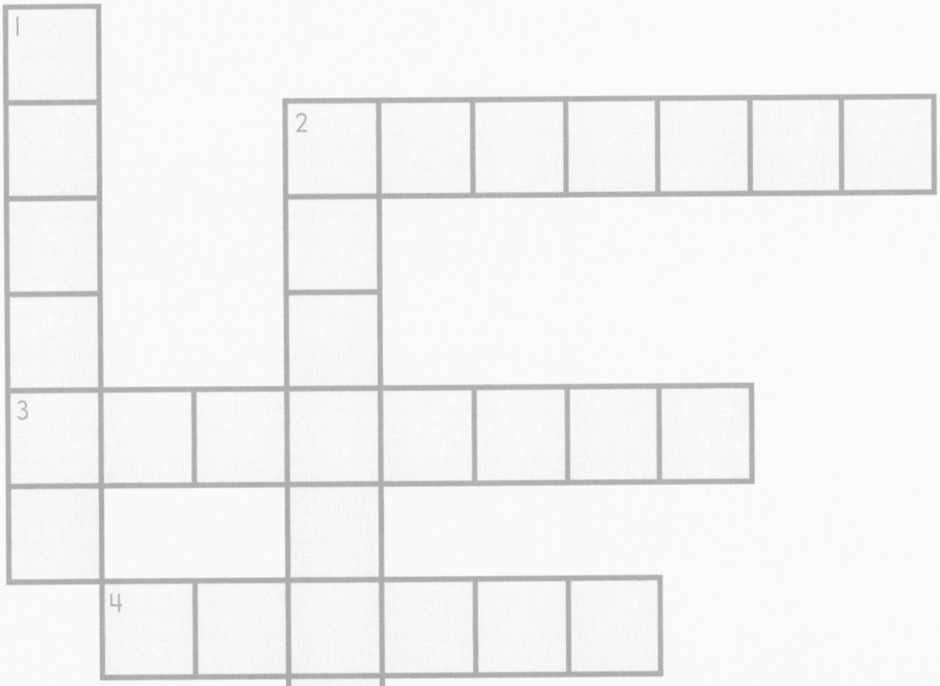

Counting & Numbering to 20

Hidden Design

COUNT the dots. Then COLOR the squares to see the hidden design.

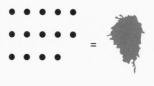
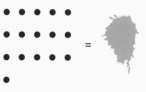

16	16	16	16	16	16	16	13
19	19	19	19	19	19	13	16
17	17	17	17	17	13	19	16
12	12	12	12	13	17	19	16
14	14	14	13	12	17	19	16
18	18	13	14	12	17	19	16
11	13	18	14	12	17	19	16
13	11	18	14	12	17	19	16

Ant Farm

The signs are in the wrong places. DRAW a line from each sign to the ant farm where it belongs.

15 Ants

16 Ants

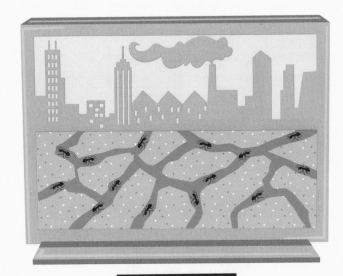

18 Ants

14 Ants

Safe Crackers

WRITE the sums. Then WRITE the sums from smallest to largest to find the right combination for the safe.

7	10	3	6	9	8
+ 8	+ 10	+ 9	+ 5	+ 9	+ 6

1   2   3   4   5   6

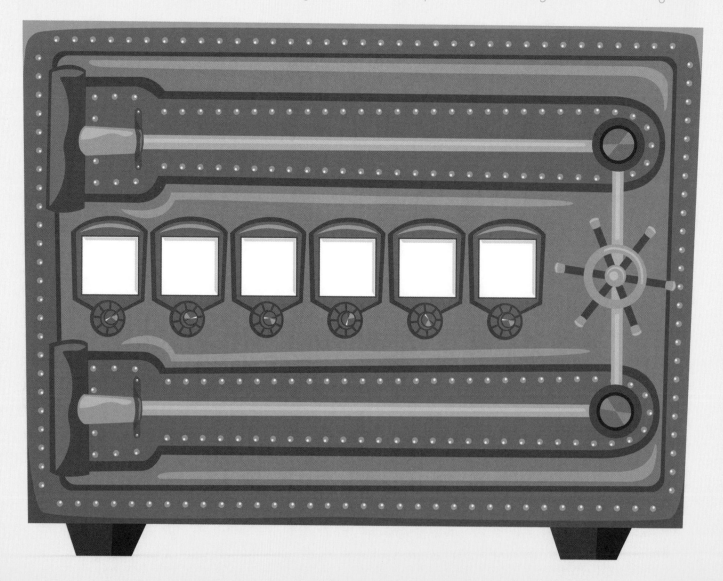

Spin It

Use the spinner from page 114. SPIN the spinner once for each problem, and WRITE the number in the blue box. Then WRITE the sum in the red box. (Save the spinner to use again.)

9 + ⬜ = ⬜   ⬜ + 7 = ⬜

⬜ + 10 = ⬜   6 + ⬜ = ⬜

8 + ⬜ = ⬜   ⬜ + 9 = ⬜

⬜ + 7 = ⬜   10 + ⬜ = ⬜

6 + ⬜ = ⬜   ⬜ + 8 = ⬜

Your Deal

Using the number cards 2 through 10 from a deck of playing cards, DEAL a card onto each space. SAY the sum out loud. REPEAT until you have run out of cards.

 + = ?

 + = ?

Code Breaker

SOLVE each problem. Then WRITE the letter that matches each sum to solve the riddle.

9 + 4 1 **H**	11 + 8 2 **V**	5 + 6 3 **I**	8 + 7 4 **A**	14 + 4 5 **M**	10 +10 6 **O**

12 + 2 7 **T**	6 + 6 8 **E**	7 + 9 9 **S**

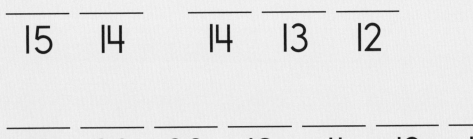

Where did the cow
spend her afternoon?

‾‾‾ ‾‾‾   ‾‾‾ ‾‾‾ ‾‾‾
 15   14   14   13   12

‾‾‾ ‾‾‾ ‾‾‾ ‾‾‾ ‾‾‾ ‾‾‾ ‾‾‾ !
 18   20   20   19   11   12   16

Domino Dots

Using the dominoes from pages 109 and 111, PLACE one domino in each blue space. WRITE the total number of dots on each domino, and then WRITE the sum of the dots on both dominoes.

Crossing Paths

WRITE the missing numbers.

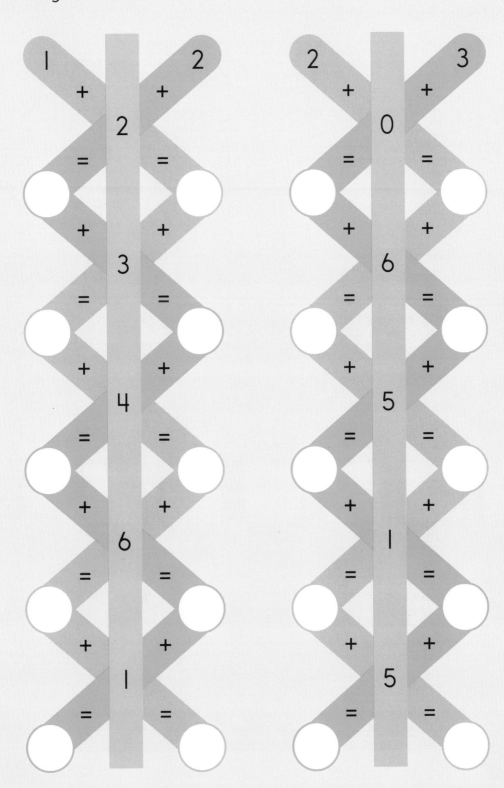

Safe Crackers

WRITE the differences. Then WRITE the differences from largest to smallest to find the right combination for the safe.

19	14	11	20	16	13
− 7	− 8	− 2	− 2	−11	−12
1	2	3	4	5	6

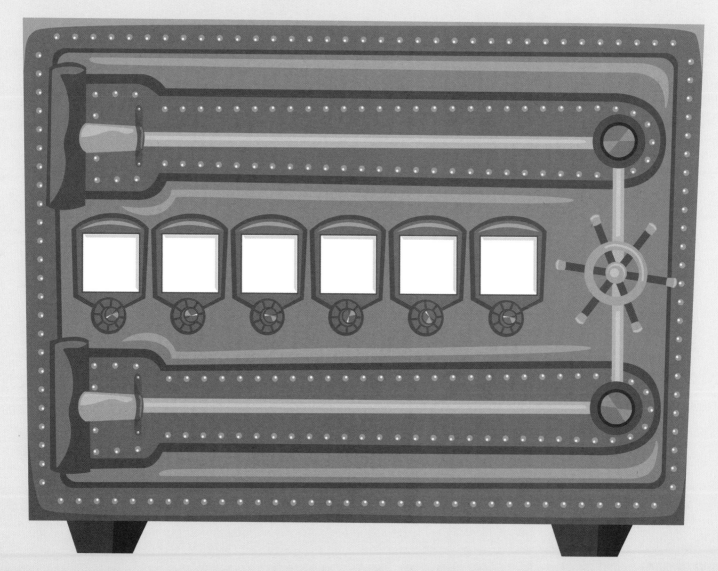

Spin It

Use the spinner from page 114. SPIN the spinner once for each problem, and WRITE the number in the yellow box. Then WRITE the difference in the blue box. (Save the spinner to use again.)

13 − ☐ = ☐   16 − ☐ = ☐

20 − ☐ = ☐   11 − ☐ = ☐

15 − ☐ = ☐   14 − ☐ = ☐

18 − ☐ = ☐   12 − ☐ = ☐

19 − ☐ = ☐   17 − ☐ = ☐

Subtracting Differences from 20

Missing Middles

WRITE the number missing from the center square.

1.

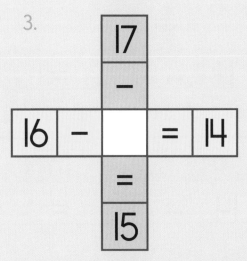

$$15 - \boxed{}$$
$$11 - \boxed{} = 3$$
$$= 7$$

2.

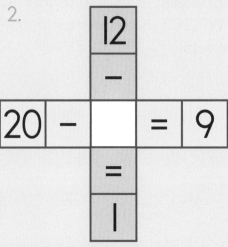

$$12 - \boxed{}$$
$$20 - \boxed{} = 9$$
$$= 1$$

3.

$$17 - \boxed{}$$
$$16 - \boxed{} = 14$$
$$= 15$$

4.

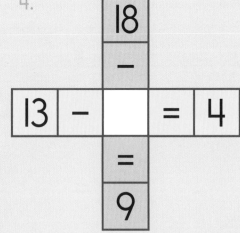

$$18 - \boxed{}$$
$$13 - \boxed{} = 4$$
$$= 9$$

5.

$$20 - \boxed{}$$
$$19 - \boxed{} = 4$$
$$= 5$$

6.

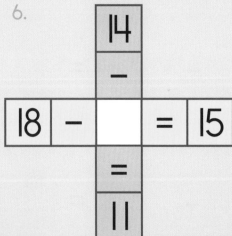

$$14 - \boxed{}$$
$$18 - \boxed{} = 15$$
$$= 11$$

Crossing Paths

WRITE the missing numbers.

20   18   17   19

-3 $-$ -1 $-$

$=$ $=$ $=$ $=$

$\bigcirc$ $\bigcirc$ $\bigcirc$ $\bigcirc$

-2 $-$ -4 $-$

$=$ $=$ $=$ $=$

$\bigcirc$ $\bigcirc$ $\bigcirc$ $\bigcirc$

-5 $-$ -2 $-$

$=$ $=$ $=$ $=$

$\bigcirc$ $\bigcirc$ $\bigcirc$ $\bigcirc$

-0 $-$ -6 $-$

$=$ $=$ $=$ $=$

$\bigcirc$ $\bigcirc$ $\bigcirc$ $\bigcirc$

-7 $-$ -4 $-$

$=$ $=$ $=$ $=$

$\bigcirc$ $\bigcirc$ $\bigcirc$ $\bigcirc$

31

Subtracting Differences from 20

Pipe Down

WRITE the missing number. Then FOLLOW the pipe, and WRITE the same number in the next problem.

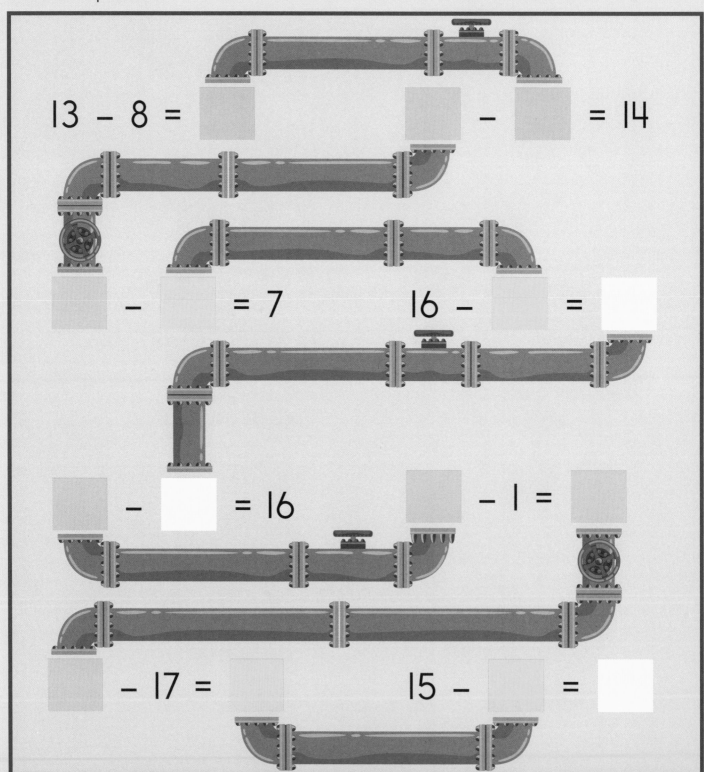

13 − 8 = ☐   ☐ − ☐ = 14

☐ − ☐ = 7   16 − ☐ = ☐

☐ − ☐ = 16   ☐ − 1 = ☐

☐ − 17 = ☐   15 − ☐ = ☐

Space Walk

Using the numbers in the picture, WRITE as many fact families with the number 17 as you can.

☐ + ☐ = ☐

☐ + ☐ = ☐

☐ − ☐ = ☐

☐ − ☐ = ☐

☐ + ☐ = ☐

☐ + ☐ = ☐

☐ − ☐ = ☐

☐ − ☐ = ☐

☐ + ☐ = ☐

☐ + ☐ = ☐

☐ − ☐ = ☐

☐ − ☐ = ☐

Magic Square

WRITE the numbers 1 through 9 in the square so that every group of three numbers across, down, and diagonally has a sum of 15.

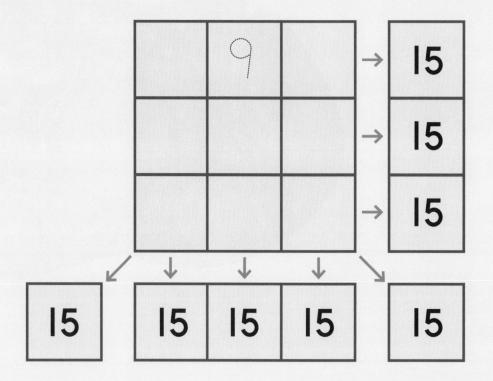

Crossing Paths

WRITE the missing numbers.

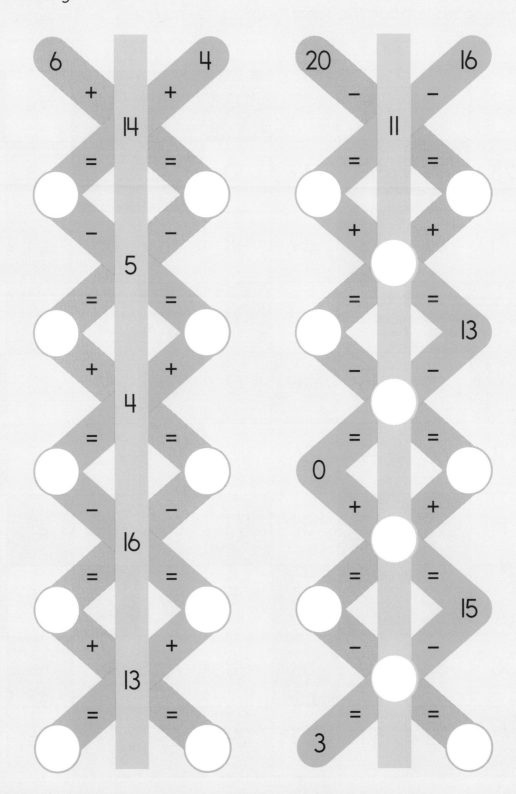

Color Mix-up

These squares are all the right colors, but they're in the wrong order. COLOR the squares on the opposite page the same color as the numbers on this page to see the design.

45	52	8	81	17	93	37	14	61	28
18	23	79	58	72	30	78	51	13	80
60	71	67	22	89	48	35	86	68	94
9	46	96	26	1	34	65	41	100	16
88	74	19	85	95	73	57	87	29	77
27	4	66	49	36	15	99	2	47	59
33	11	92	12	31	43	84	64	25	7
76	53	3	62	50	5	55	21	56	97
42	38	82	70	63	90	75	44	91	40
10	98	32	54	20	24	83	39	6	69

1	2	3	4	5	6	7	8	9	10
11	12	13	14	15	16	17	18	19	20
21	22	23	24	25	26	27	28	29	30
31	32	33	34	35	36	37	38	39	40
41	42	43	44	45	46	47	48	49	50
51	52	53	54	55	56	57	58	59	60
61	62	63	64	65	66	67	68	69	70
71	72	73	74	75	76	77	78	79	80
81	82	83	84	85	86	87	88	89	90
91	92	93	94	95	96	97	98	99	100

Counting to 100

Super Spies

WRITE the missing numbers in the chart. DECODE the note on the opposite page, using the letters in those squares.

	O							C	
1	2	3	4	5	6	7	8		10
	L	T					N		
11	12			15	16	17		19	20
21	22	23	24	25	26	27	28	29	30
					P				E
31	32	33	34	35		37	38	39	
	S								
41		43	44	45	46	47	48	49	50
			V					I	
51	52	53		55	56	57	58		60
K						H			
	62	63	64	65	66		68	69	70
71	72	73	74	75	76	77	78	79	80
				A					
81	82	83	84		86	87	88	89	90
R									D
	92	93	94	95	96	97	98	99	

14   67   40   42   40   9   91   40   14

36   13   85   18   42   85   91   40

67   59   100   100   40   18   59   18

14   67   40   54   85   42   40

○
2   18   14   67   40

100   40   42   61 .

Hidden Design

COUNT the tens and ones. Then COLOR the squares that match the numbers to see the hidden design.

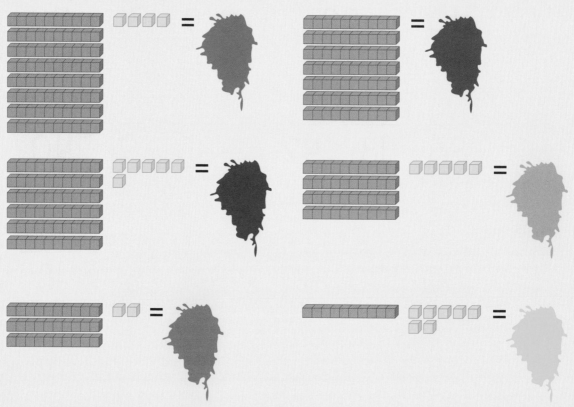

66	66	66	66	66	66	66	66
66	84	84	84	84	84	84	84
84	84	17	17	17	17	17	17
17	17	17	45	45	45	45	45
45	45	45	45	32	32	32	32
32	32	32	32	32	70	70	70
70	70	70	70	70	70	66	66
66	66	66	66	66	66	66	84

Safe Crackers

WRITE the number for each picture. Then WRITE the digit in the tens place of each number from largest to smallest to find the combination for the safe.

1. 43

2.

3.

4.

5.

6.

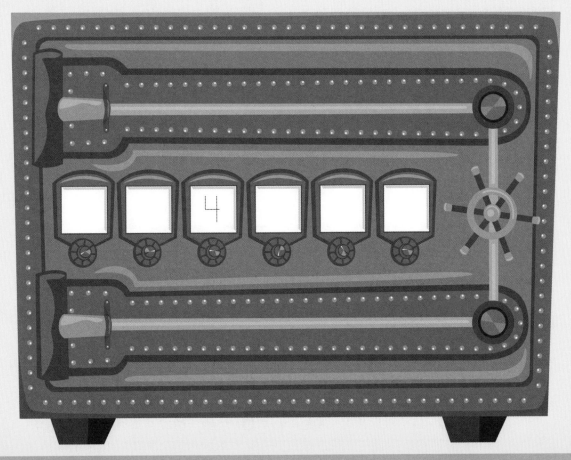

Number Search

WRITE the number for each picture. Then CIRCLE it in the puzzle.

HINT: Numbers are across and down only.

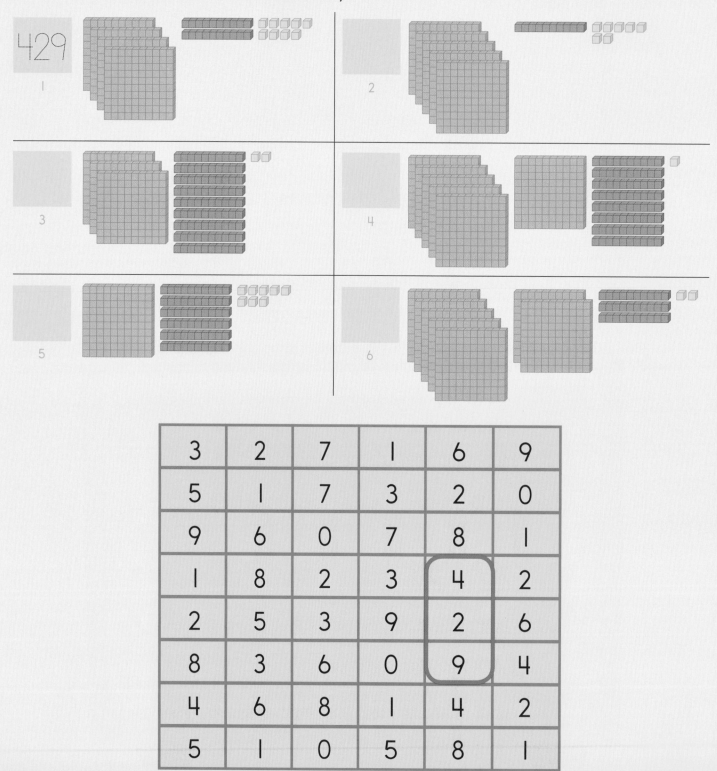

8

Code Breaker

WRITE the number for each picture. Then WRITE the letter that matches each number to solve the riddle.

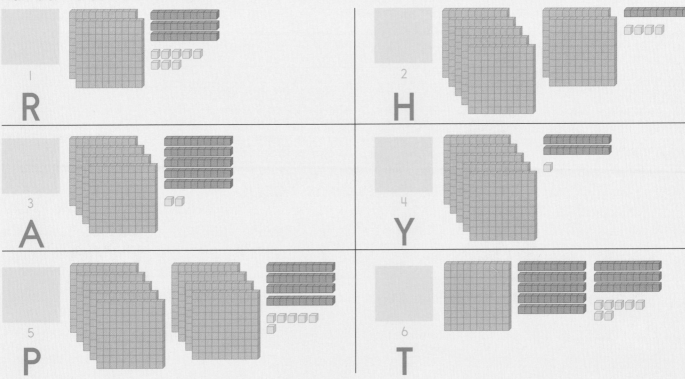

1 **R**

2 **H**

3 **A**

4 **Y**

5 **P**

6 **T**

What did the pirate wear to his birthday party?

___
452

___ ___ ___ ___ ___ ___ ___
946 452 238 238 238 187 521

___ ___ ___.
714 452 187

43

Stepping Stones

START at the arrow. DRAW a path by counting up from 53 to reach the bunny.

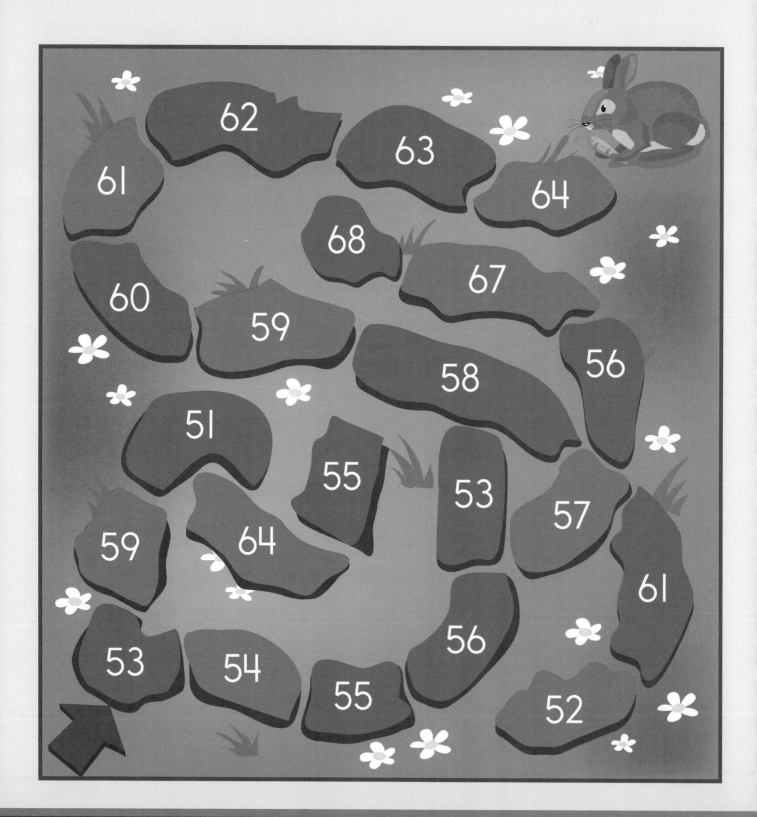

Where's My Brain?

START at the arrow. DRAW a path by skip counting by 2 to reach the brain.

HINT: Skip counting is like adding 2 to each number. For example: 1, 3, 5, 7, and so on.

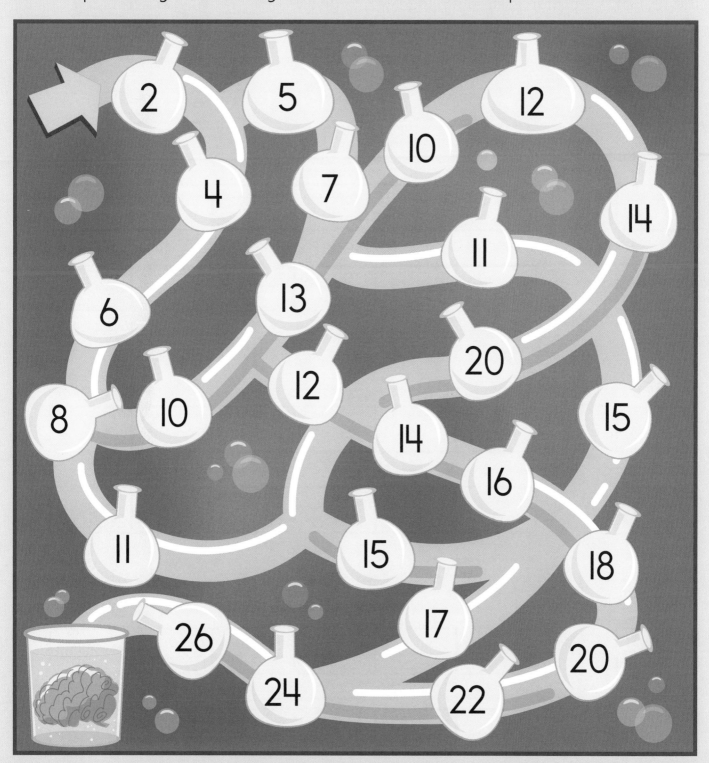

Spin It

Use the spinner from page 114. SPIN the spinner, and WRITE the number in the first box. Then WRITE the rest of the pattern, skip counting by 2, 5, or 10. (Save the spinner to use again.)

Skip count by 2:

Skip count by 5:

Skip count by 10:

Roll It

ROLL a number cube, and WRITE the number in the first box. ROLL it again and write the number in the second box. Then WRITE the next six numbers, skip counting by the difference between the first two numbers.

Example:

+3   +3

| 2 | 5 | 8 | 11 | 14 | 17 | 20 | 23 |

| | | | | | | | |

| | | | | | | | |

| | | | | | | | |

| | | | | | | | |

| | | | | | | | |

Find the Fountain

START at the arrow, and DRAW the correct path to the center fountain.
When there is a choice of numbers, follow the smaller number.

Just Right

WRITE each number next to a smaller blue number.

HINT: There may be more than one place to put a number, but you need to use every number.

28 71 55 83 20 46 66 12 99 76

13 20
1

58
3

93
5

46
7

75
9

67
2

4
4

22
6

80
8

31
10

49

Find the Fountain

START at the arrow, and DRAW the correct path to the center fountain.
When there is a choice of numbers, follow the larger number.

Win Big

Wherever two boxes point to one box, WRITE the larger number. START at the sides and work toward the center to see which number will win big.

Cool Combinations

WRITE all of the different possible three-digit numbers you can make from the numbers 2, 3, and 6. Then CIRCLE the largest number.

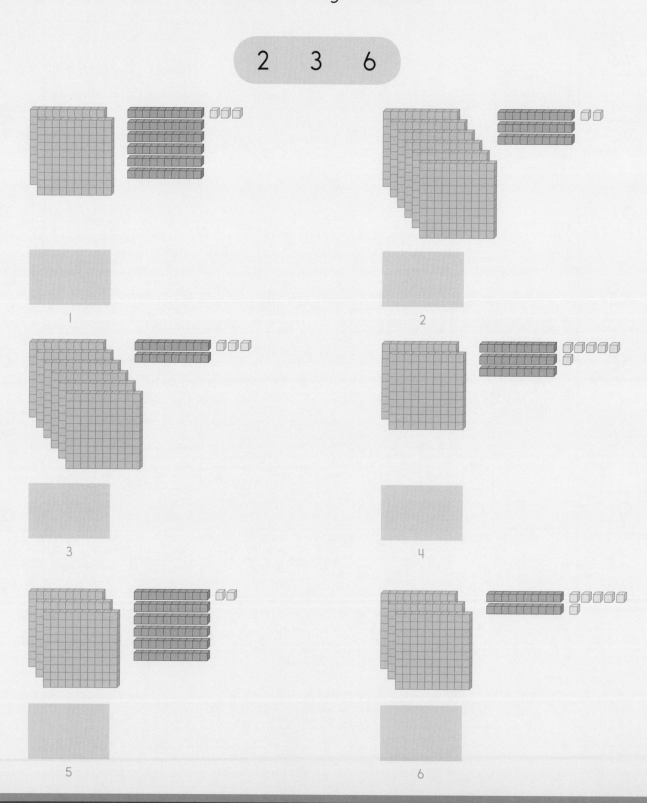

Skip to My Loo

SKIP COUNT by 2, 3, 4, and 5, and WRITE the numbers along each track.

Skip count by:

2	3	4	5
1	1	1	1
3			

Finish

Picture Perfect

DRAW different size rectangles to make buildings. Then DRAW doors and windows and COLOR the buildings.

Hidden Shapes

FIND each shape hidden in the picture. DRAW a line to connect each shape with its location in the picture.

Doodle Pad

TRACE the shapes. Then DRAW a picture using each shape.

Trap the Circle

CONNECT the eight dots to draw one square inside the circle and one square outside the circle. Do not lift your pencil, and do not trace over any line already drawn.

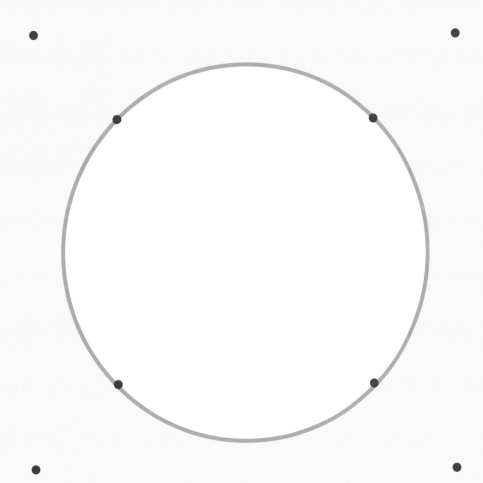

Turns and Transformations

CUT OUT the 12 cards on page 59, and ARRANGE them to make each shape shown on this page.

Sneaky Shapes

WRITE the number of triangles and rectangles you see.

HINT: Think about the different ways smaller shapes can make larger shapes, like when four small triangles make a larger triangle.

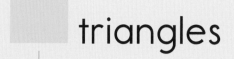 triangles

rectangles

Shape Shifters

A shape has **symmetry** if a line can divide the shape so each half is a mirror image of the other. Use the pattern block pieces from page 115, and PLACE the pieces to make each picture symmetrical without overlapping any pieces. (Save the pattern block pieces to use again.)

Incredible Illusions

COLOR the picture so it is symmetrical. When you're done coloring, LOOK at the picture. Do you see two faces or a candlestick?

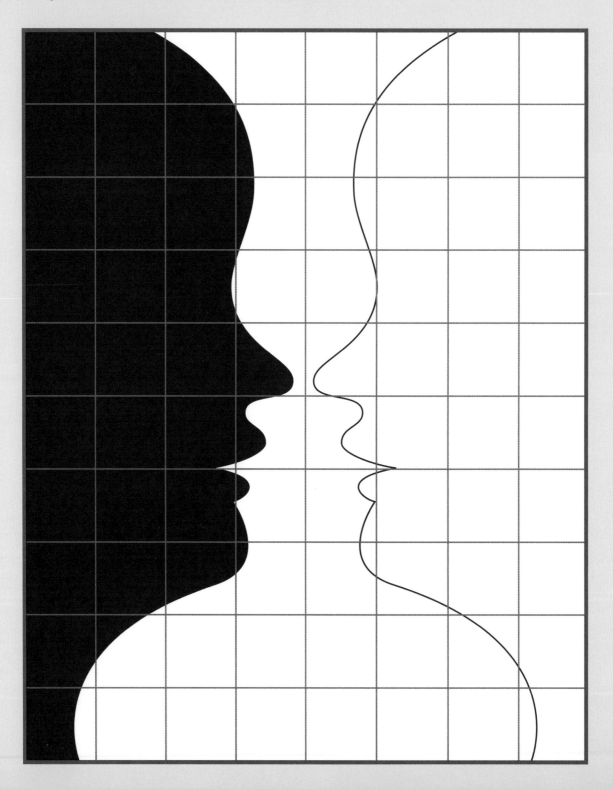

Cool Kaleidoscope

COLOR the kaleidoscope so it is symmetrical.

HINT: Work across the top, then make the bottom a mirror image of the top.

Tricky Tangrams

Use the tangram pieces from page 117, and PLACE the pieces to completely fill each shape. (Save the pieces to use again.)

HINT: Try placing the largest pieces first.

Shape Shifters

Use the pattern block pieces from page 115, and PLACE the pieces to completely fill each shape without overlapping any pieces. See if you can solve the puzzles different ways. (Save the pieces to use again.)

Odd Way Home

Michael lives in the house with a star on it, and he is playing a game on his ride home. He only wants to make right turns, and he doesn't want to ride past any red houses. DRAW a line to show his way home.

Castle Quest

The knight has been called to duty at the castle. FOLLOW the directions, and DRAW the path to the right castle.

To the castle:
Go straight four spaces.
Go left two spaces.
Go left two spaces.
Go right four spaces.
Go right two spaces.
Go left three spaces.
Go right three spaces.
Go left two spaces.

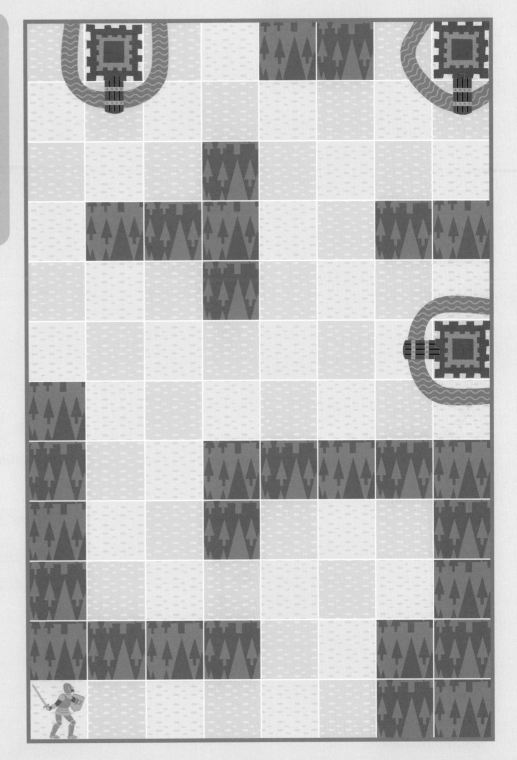

Maps

Go for a Ride

FIND each ride on the map on the opposite page. WRITE the location of each ride using the given locations.

HINT: When you find a ride on the map, follow the lines down and left to find its location letter and number.

Locations: E3   B7   A2   DI   E7   C3   A6   D5   BI

72

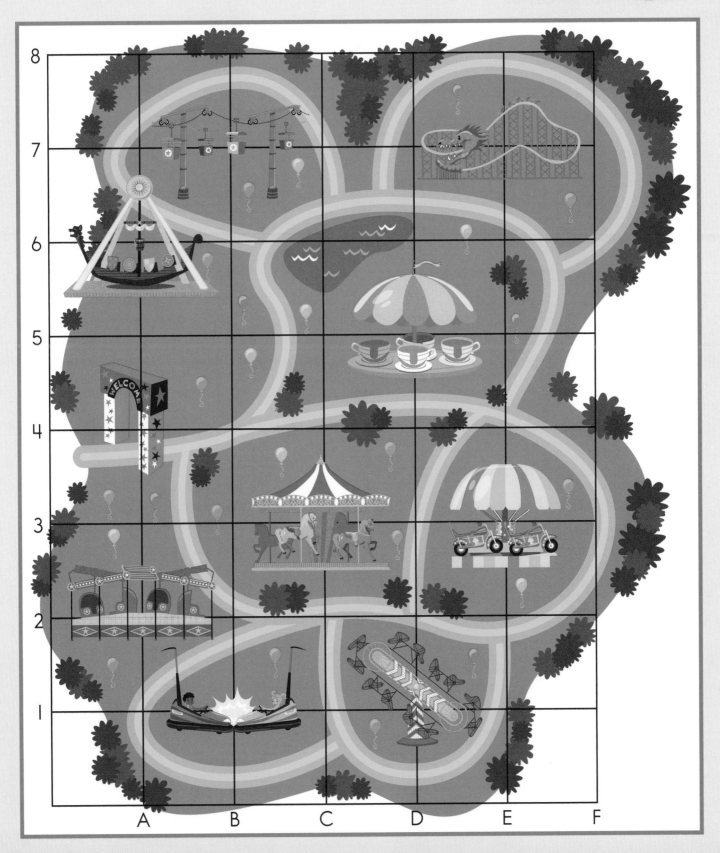

Tricky Tangrams

Use the tangram pieces from page 117, and PLACE the pieces to make this square two different ways without overlapping any pieces.

PLACE the pieces to completely fill each shape without overlapping any pieces.

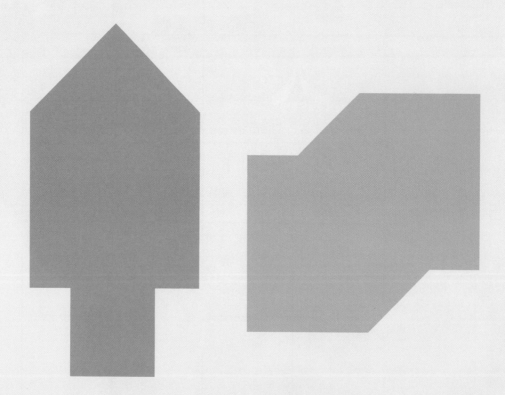

Shape Shifters

Use the pattern block pieces from page 115, and PLACE the pieces to make this shape four different ways without overlapping any pieces. Can you think of even more ways to make this shape?

PLACE the pieces to make the picture symmetrical without overlapping any pieces.

House Hunt

HUNT around your home to FIND eight things longer than this line of 5 paper clips.
WRITE what you find.

House Hunt

HUNT around your home to FIND eight things shorter than this line of 10 ants.
WRITE what you find.

_____

_____

_____

_____

_____

_____

Caterpillar Coins

Each caterpillar is four coins long. MEASURE each caterpillar with a line of four quarters, dimes, nickels, and pennies. When you find a match, WRITE the name of the coin.

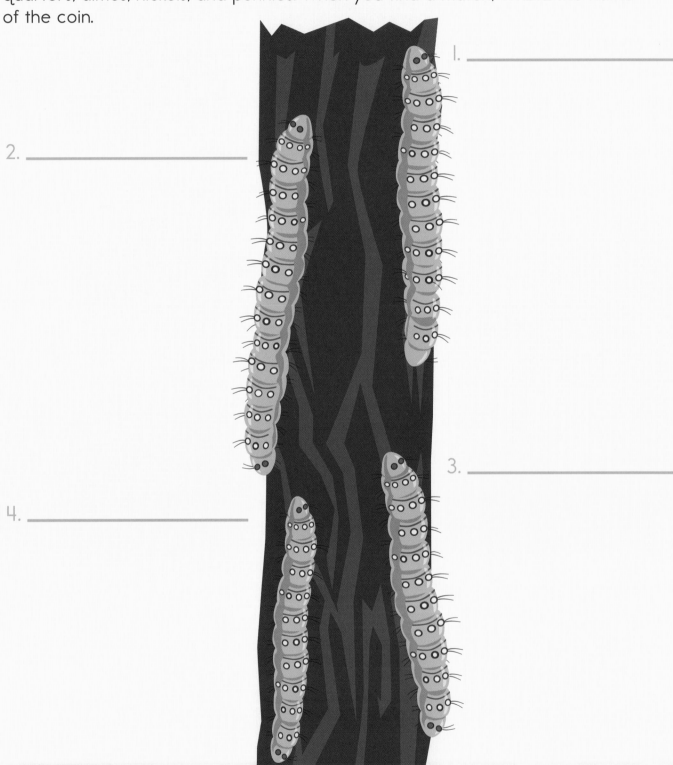

1. _____

2. _____

3. _____

4. _____

Picking Pairs

LINE UP pennies and MEASURE each wand. DRAW a line connecting pairs of wands that are the same length.

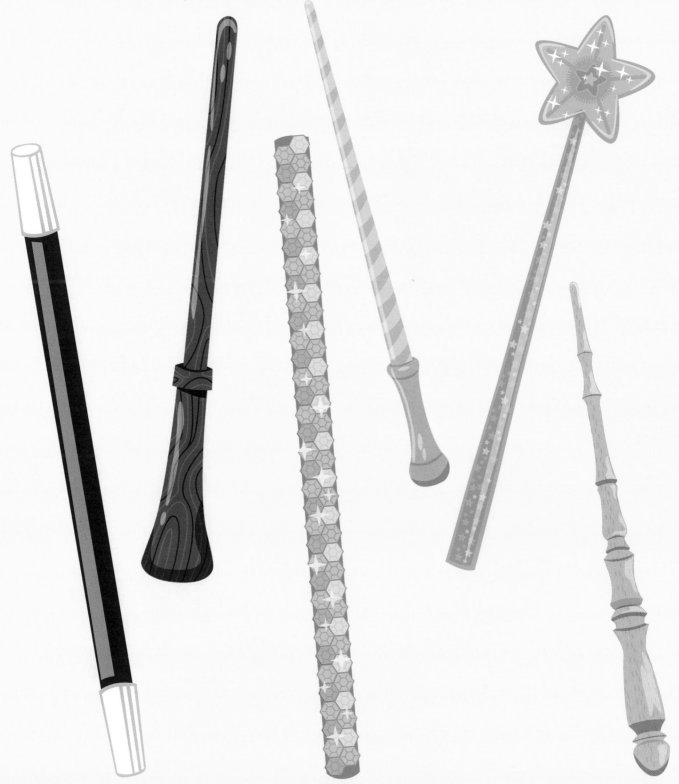

Code Ruler

MEASURE the line in inches. WRITE the letter that appears at each measurement to answer the riddle.

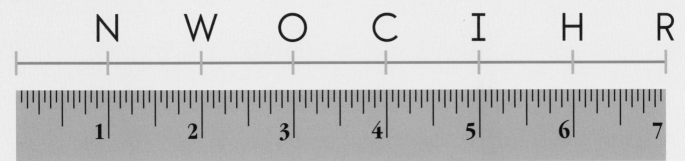

N   W   O   C   I   H   R

What kind of animal loves rulers?

An ___ ___ ___ ___ ___ ___ ___ M.
5 in. 1 in. 4 in. 6 in. 2 in. 3 in. 7 in.

Basket of Fries

One french fry in the basket is not the same length as the others. MEASURE each french fry in inches, and CIRCLE the one that is **not** the same length.

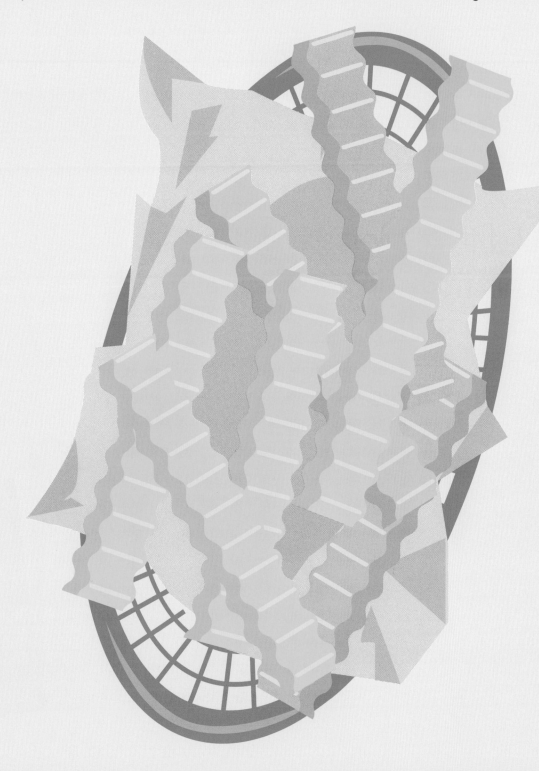

Code Ruler

MEASURE the line in centimeters. WRITE the letter that appears at each measurement to answer the riddle.

What did the ruler say when he left his friends?

___ ___   ___ ___ ___ ___!
8 cm 15 cm   3 cm 15 cm 5 cm 13 cm

Toothy the Shark

MEASURE the length of each tooth in centimeters. DRAW lines connecting pairs of teeth that are the same length.

Coming Closest

WRITE the numbers 1 through 6 on the asteroids so that 1 is the asteroid you think is closest to the planet and 6 is the asteroid you think is farthest away. Then MEASURE in inches to see if you're correct.

Incredible Illusions

Does the blue line or the green line look longer? CIRCLE the line that looks longer in each pair. Then MEASURE each line in inches to compare.

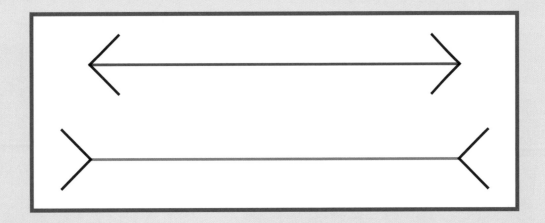

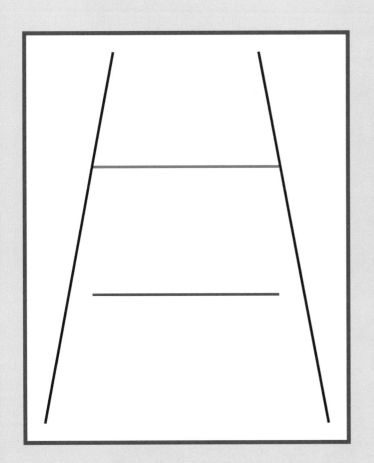

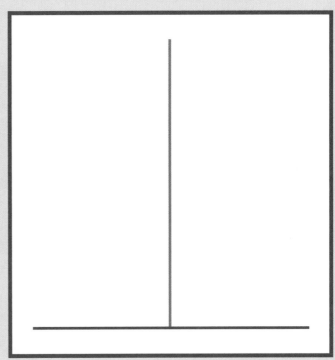

Approximation & Estimation

So Far Away

WRITE the numbers 1 through 8 next to the fireflies so that 1 is the firefly you think is closest to the light and 8 is the firefly you think is farthest away. Then MEASURE in centimeters to see if you're correct.

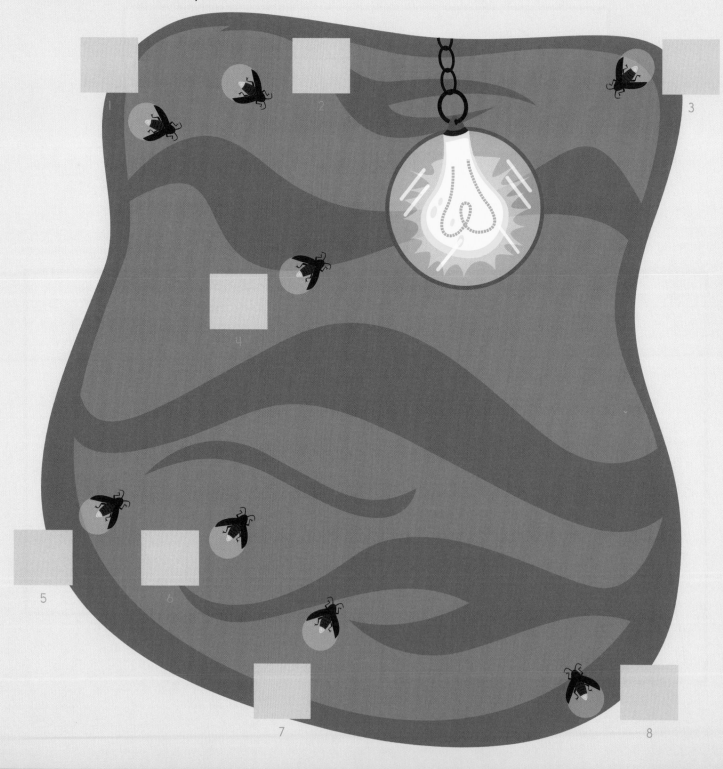

Don't Go Over

GUESS the length of each car in centimeters. Then MEASURE each car. For every centimeter in the difference between the two measurements, COLOR a section in the gas meter. If you get through the whole page without filling the gas meter, you win!

HINT: To find the difference, subtract the smaller number from the larger number.

FULL

1. Guess: _____
   Check: _____

2. Guess: _____
   Check: _____

3. Guess: _____
   Check: _____

4. Guess: _____
   Check: _____

5. Guess: _____
   Check: _____

6. Guess: _____
   Check: _____

EMPTY

Needle in a Haystack

CIRCLE the needle that is two inches long.

Don't Go Over

GUESS the distance between each pair of bugs in centimeters. Then MEASURE the distance. For every centimeter in the difference between the two measurements, COLOR a section on the chart. If you get through the whole page without filling the chart, you win!

HINT: To find the difference, subtract the smaller number from the larger number.

1. Guess: _____   Check: _____

2. Guess: _____   Check: _____

3. Guess: _____   Check: _____

4. Guess: _____   Check: _____

5. Guess: _____   Check: _____

Mystery Time

COLOR the times in the picture according to the color of the clocks at the top.
When you are done coloring, WRITE the mystery time under the picture.

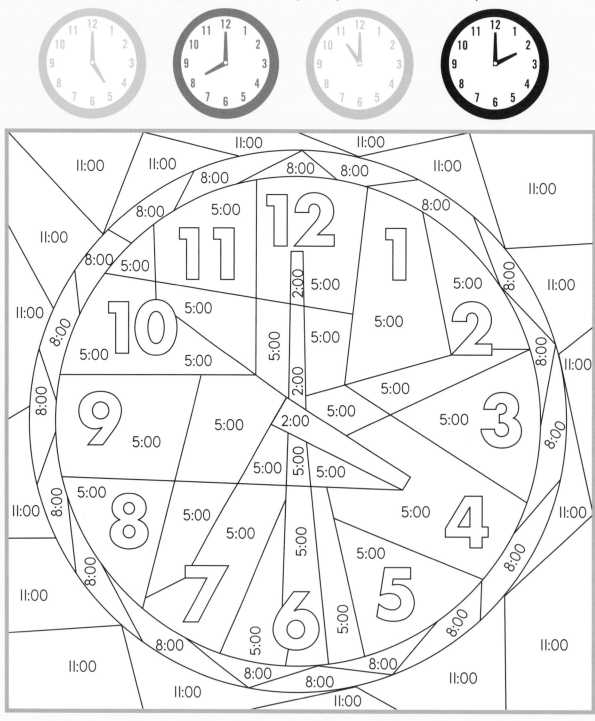

:00

Make a Match

CUT OUT the times and clocks. READ the rules. PLAY the game!
(Save these cards for use with page 95.)

Rules: Two players
1. Place the cards face down on a table.
2. Take turns turning over two cards at a time.
3. Keep the cards when you match a clock and a time.

The player with the most matches wins!

1:00		3:00	
4:00		6:00	
7:00		9:00	
10:00		12:00	

Around the Clock

Use the clock hands from page 117 and the spinner from page 114.
SPIN the spinner, then PLACE the pieces to make that time on
the clock.

HINT: Add "o'clock" to each number you spin on the spinner to
name the time.

Mystery Time

COLOR the times in the picture according to the color of the clocks at the top. When you are done coloring, WRITE the mystery time under the picture.

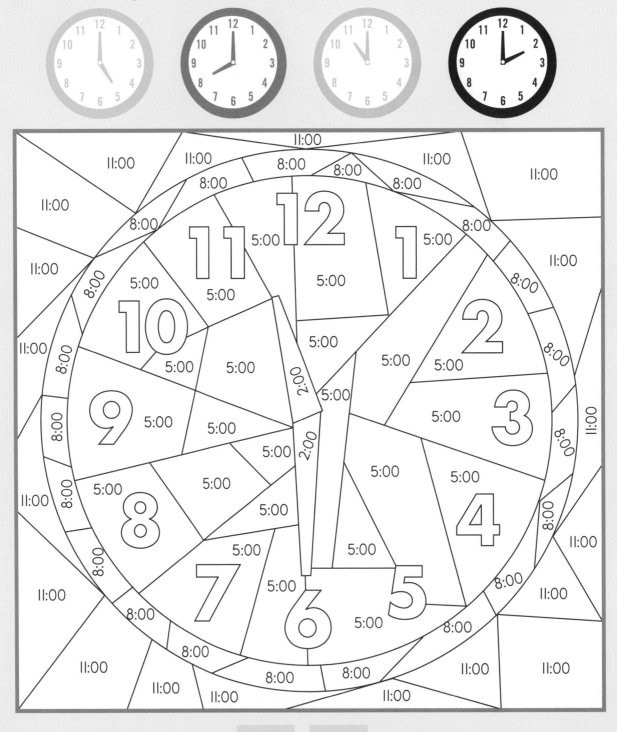

Make a Match

CUT OUT the times and clocks. READ the rules. PLAY the game!

HINT: Combine these with the cards from page 91 for a greater challenge.

Rules: Two players
1. Place the cards face down on a table.
2. Take turns turning over two cards at a time.
3. Keep the cards when you match a clock and a time.

The player with the most matches wins!

1:30		2:30	
3:30		5:30	
6:30		8:30	
11:30		12:30	

Time Travel

DRAW a line from Start through the clocks to get to the end, traveling ahead one hour as you go from clock to clock.

Start

End

What's My Time?

READ the clues, and CIRCLE the clock with the correct time.

I'm next to at least one clock that is later than I am.

I'm not usually a time when you would eat a meal.

If I'm at night, you're probably asleep.

I'm a half hour later than one of my neighbors.

Time Travel

DRAW a line from Start through the clocks to get to the end, traveling ahead two and a half hours as you go from clock to clock.

Start

End

Coin Values

Code Breaker

WRITE the value of each coin or coin set. Then WRITE the letter that matches each value to solve the riddle.

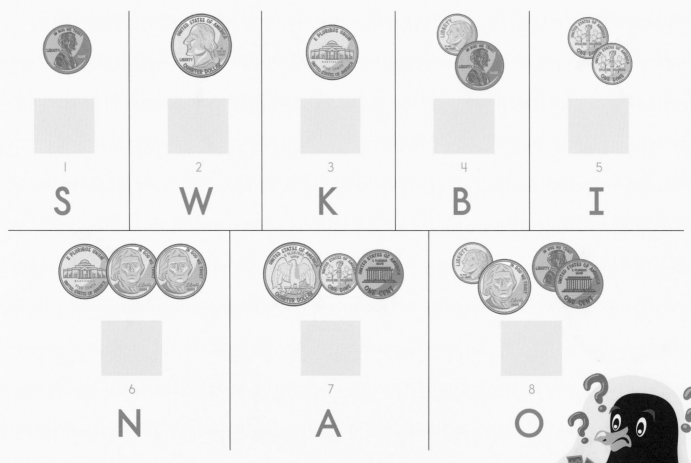

1	2	3	4	5
S	W	K	B	I

6	7	8
N	A	O

Where does the penguin keep his money?

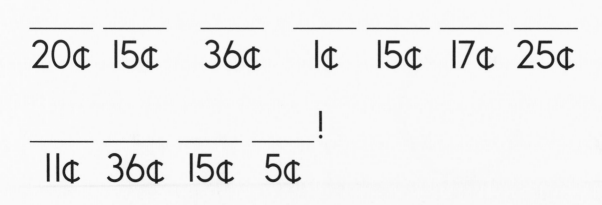

___ ___   ___   ___   ___ ___ ___
20¢ 15¢   36¢   1¢   15¢ 17¢ 25¢

___ ___ ___ ___!
11¢ 36¢ 15¢ 5¢

100

Make a Match

CUT OUT the pictures. READ the rules. PLAY the game!

Rules: Two players
1. Place the cards face down on a table.
2. Take turns turning over two cards at a time.
3. Keep the cards when you match coins with the same value.

The player with the most matches wins!

Pocket Change

DRAW exactly two lines to create four different sets of coins of equal value.

Slide Sort

CIRCLE the coins that are **not** enough money to pay for the object at the bottom of the slide.

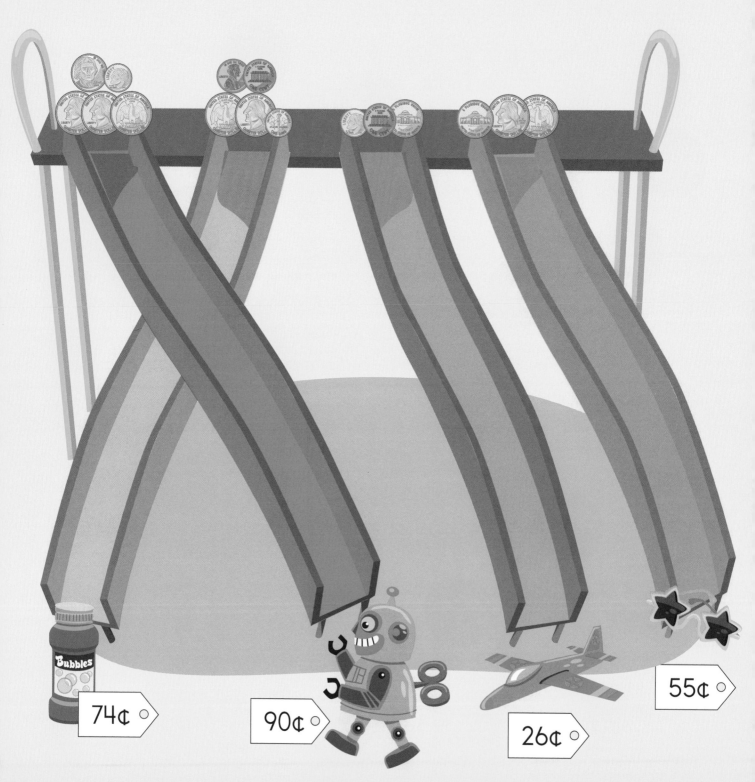

Bubbles 74¢

90¢

26¢

55¢

Make a Buck

CUT OUT the cards. READ the rules. PLAY the game!

Rules: Two players
1. Place the cards face down in a stack on a table.
2. Take turns picking a card.
3. Keep turning cards until your coins total one dollar or more.
   How many different ways can you make a dollar?

The first player to make a dollar wins!

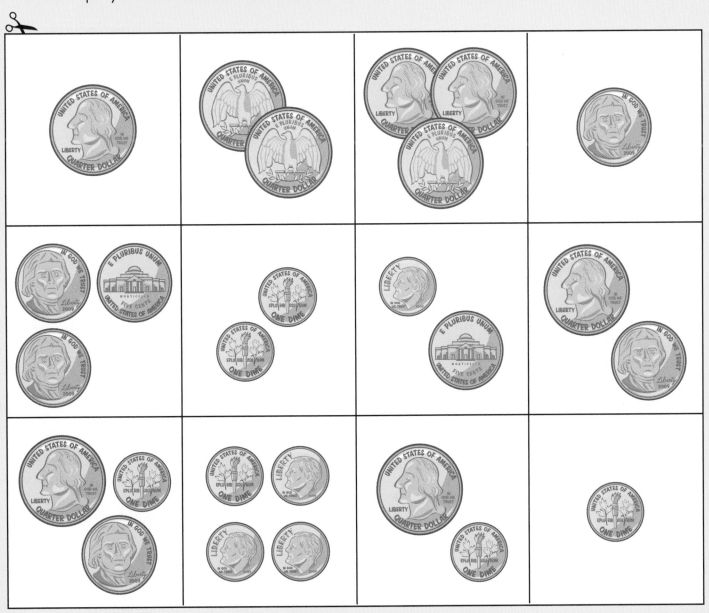

Money Maze

DRAW a line to get from the start of the maze to the end, crossing exactly enough coins to total the end amount.

HINT: There's more than one way through the maze, but you must follow the path that totals 82¢.

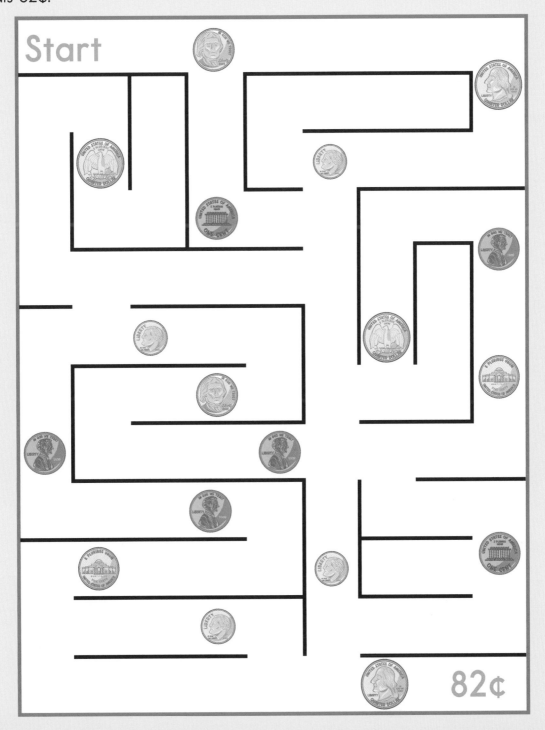

Challenge Puzzle

Money Maze

DRAW a line to get from the start of the maze to the end, crossing exactly enough coins to total the end amount.

HINT: There's more than one way through the maze, but you must follow the path that totals 99¢.

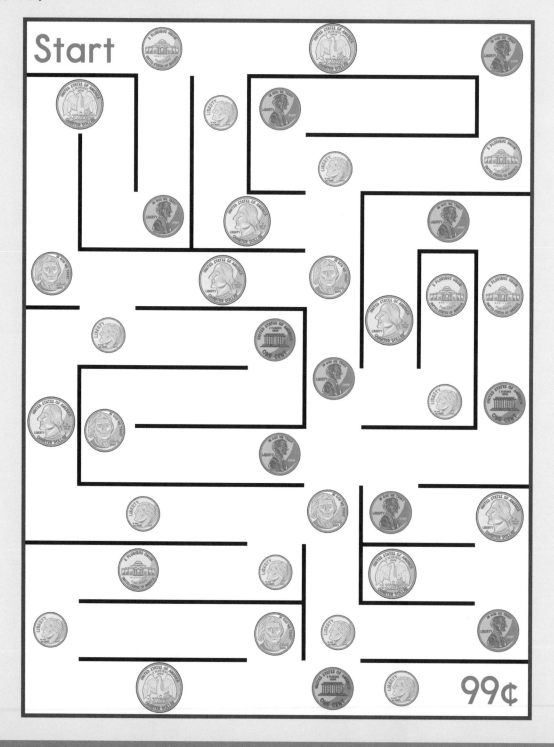

Start

99¢

Dominoes

CUT OUT the dominoes.

These dominoes are for use with pages 4 and 26.

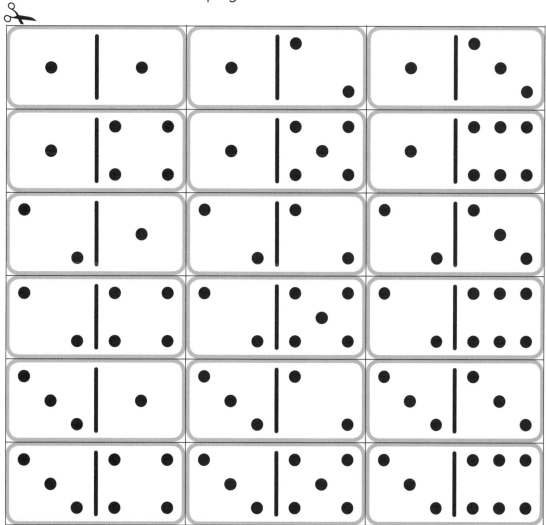

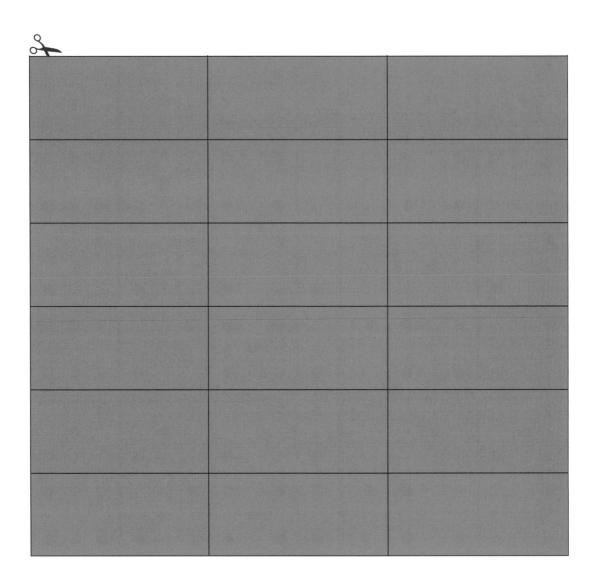

Dominoes

CUT OUT the dominoes.

These dominoes are for use with pages 4 and 26.

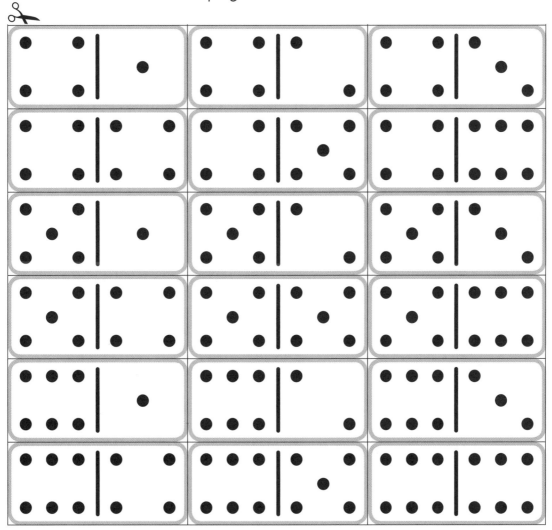

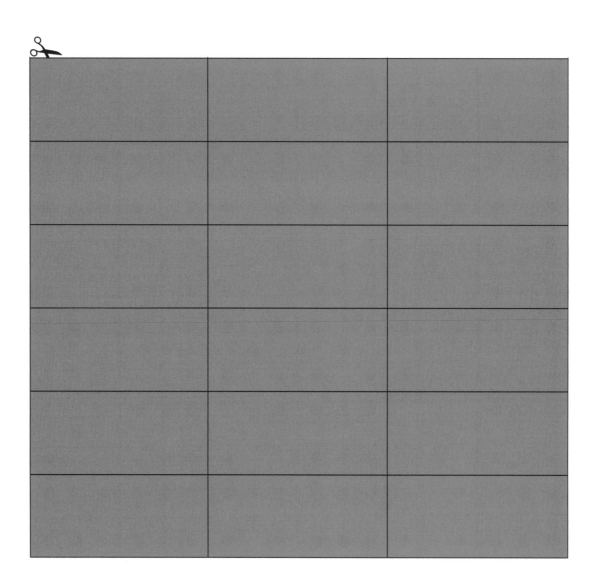

Spinners

CUT OUT the spinner. BEND the outer part of a paper clip so that it points out, and carefully POKE it through the center dot of the spinner. You're ready to spin!

This spinner is for use with pages 7 and 12, and the reverse side is for use with pages 23, 29, 46, and 93.

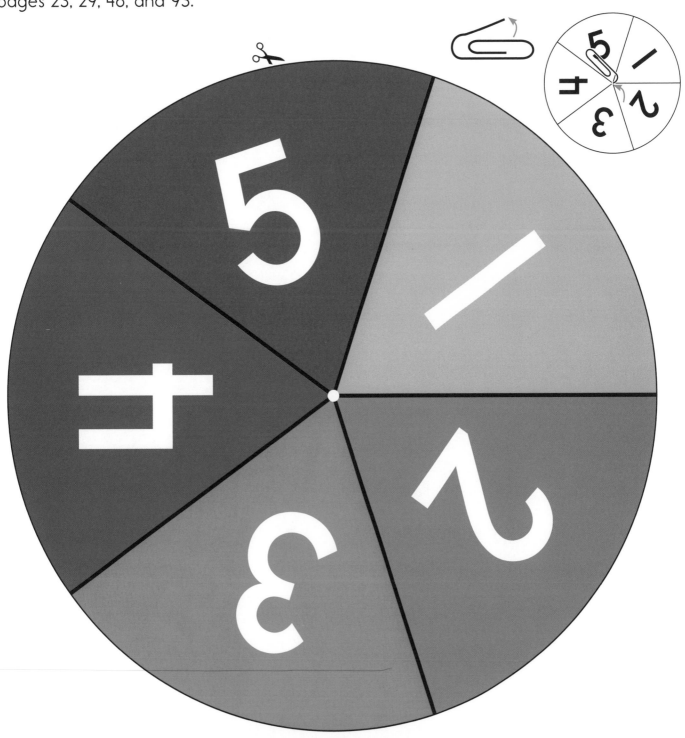

Game Pieces

Use the spinner on this side for pages 23, 29, 46, and 93. Pull out the paper clip from the other side, and poke it through the center dot on this side.

Pattern Blocks

CUT OUT the 31 pattern block pieces.

These pattern block pieces are for use with pages 62, 63, 68, 69, and 75.

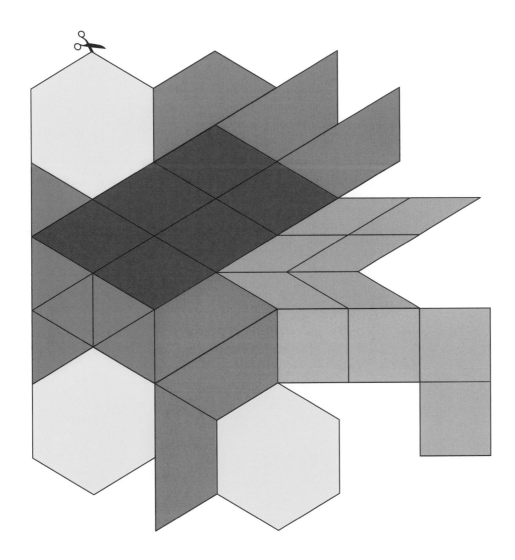

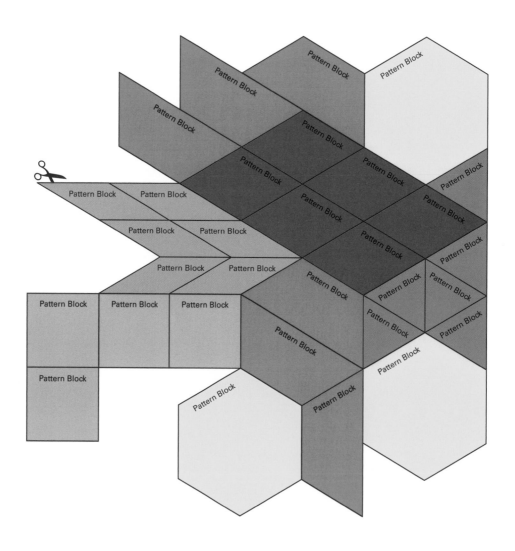

Tangrams

CUT OUT the seven tangram pieces.

These tangram pieces are for use with pages 66, 67, and 74.

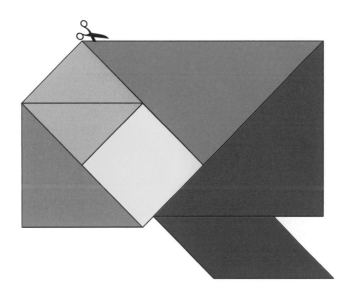

Clock Hands

CUT OUT the clock hands. These clock hands are for use with page 93.

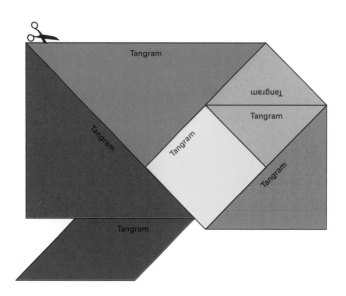

Answers

Page 2

Page 3

Page 4
Have someone check
your answers.

Page 5
1. 7   2. 6
3. 5   4. 2
5. 9   6. 8
Combination: 2 5 6 7 8 9

Page 6
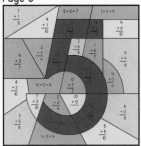

Page 7
Have someone check
your answers.

Page 8
Have someone check
your answers.

Page 9
1. 4   2. 10
3. 9   4. 6
5. 8   6. 1
7. 5   8. 7
9. 3
BECAUSE 7 8 9!

Page 10
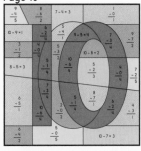

Page 11
1. 2   2. 4
3. 3   4. 8
5. 6   6. 0
Combination: 8 6 4 3 2 0

Page 12
Have someone check
your answers.

Page 13
1. 5   2. 1
3. 4   4. 2
5. 0   6. 7

Page 14
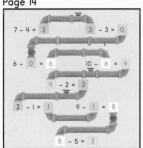

Page 15
8 + 1 = 9
1 + 8 = 9
9 − 8 = 1
9 − 1 = 8

5 + 4 = 9
4 + 5 = 9
9 − 5 = 4
9 − 4 = 5

6 + 3 = 9
3 + 6 = 9
9 − 6 = 3
9 − 3 = 6

Page 16

Page 17
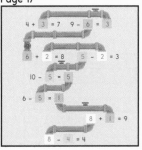

Page 18

Page 19
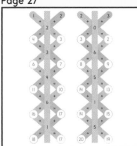

Page 20
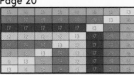

Page 21
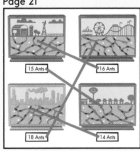

Page 22
1. 15   2. 20
3. 12   4. 11
5. 18   6. 14
Combination: 11 12 14 15 18 20

Page 23
Have someone check
your answers.

Page 24
Have someone check
your answers.

Page 25
1. 13   2. 19
3. 11   4. 15
5. 18   6. 20
7. 14   8. 12
9. 16
AT THE MOOVIES!

Page 26
Have someone check
your answers.

Page 27
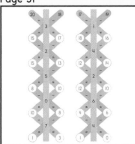

Page 28
1. 12   2. 6
3. 9   4. 18
5. 5   6. 1
Combination: 18 12 9 6 5 1

Page 29
Have someone check
your answers.

Page 30
1. 8   2. 11
3. 2   4. 9
5. 15   6. 3

Page 31
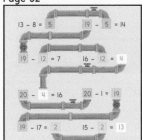

Page 32

Answers

Page 33
11 + 6 = 17
6 + 11 = 17
17 – 11 = 6
17 – 6 = 11

15 + 2 = 17
2 + 15 = 17
17 – 15 = 2
17 – 2 = 15

14 + 3 = 17
3 + 14 = 17
17 – 14 = 3
17 – 3 = 14

Page 34
Suggestion:

2	9	4
7	5	3
6	1	8

Page 35

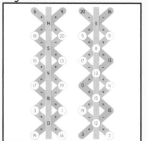

Pages 36–37

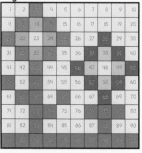

Pages 38–39
THE SECRET PLANS ARE HIDDEN IN THE VASE ON THE DESK.

Page 40

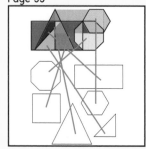

Page 41
1. 43   2. 18
3. 52   4. 61
5. 36   6. 29
Combination: 6 5 4 3 2 1

Page 42
1. 429   2. 517
3. 392   4. 681
5. 168   6. 732

3	2	7	1	6	9
5	1	7	3	2	0
9	6	0	7	8	1
1	8	2	3	4	2
2	5	3	9	2	6
8	3	6	0	9	4
4	6	8	1	4	2
5	1	0	5	8	1

Page 43
1. 238   2. 714
3. 452   4. 521
5. 946   6. 187
A PARRRTY HAT.

Page 44

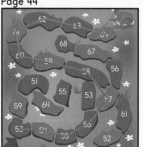

Page 45

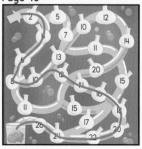

Page 46
Have someone check
your answers.

Page 47
Have someone check
your answers.

Page 48

Page 49
1. 20   2. 71
3. 66   4. 12
5. 99   6. 28
7. 55   8. 83
9. 76   10. 46

Page 50

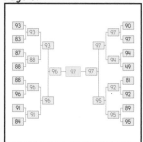

Page 51

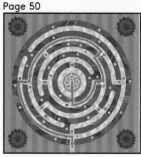

Page 52
1. 263   2. 632
3. 623   4. 236
5. 362   6. 326
Biggest number: 632

Page 53

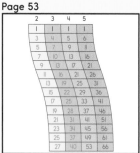

Page 54
Have someone check
your answers.

Page 55

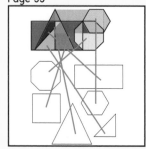

Page 56
Have someone check
your answers.

Page 57
Suggestion:
First connect the four dots on the circle to make a square.

Then connect the last dot of the square to a dot on the outside of the circle.

Finally, draw the second square around the circle.

Page 58
Have someone check
your answers.

Page 61
1. 13   2. 9

Page 62

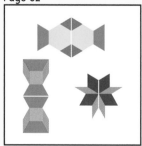

Page 63

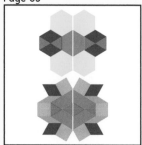

120

Page 64

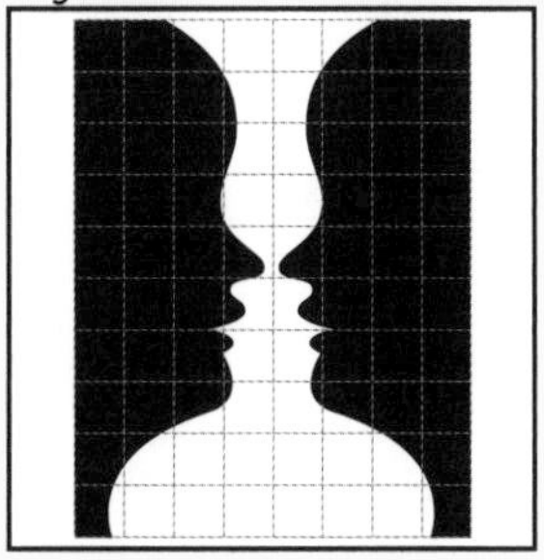

Page 65

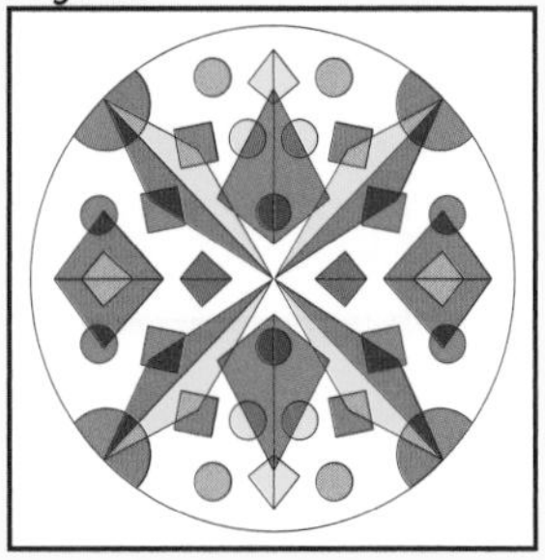

Page 66
Suggestion:

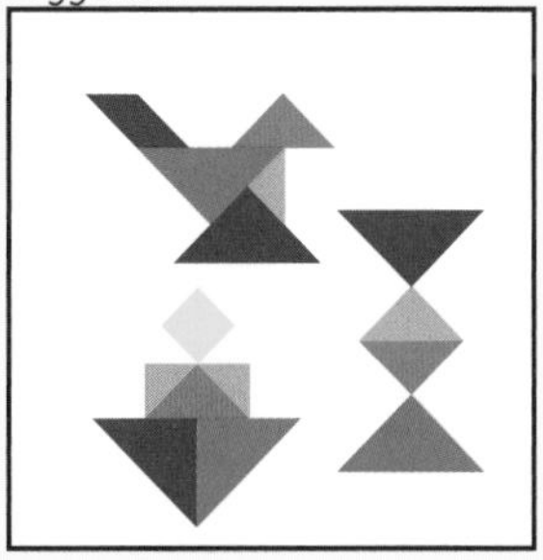

Page 67
Suggestion:

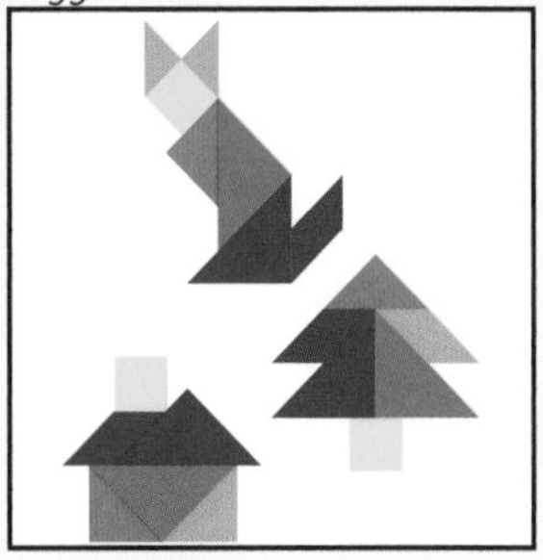

Page 68
Suggestion:

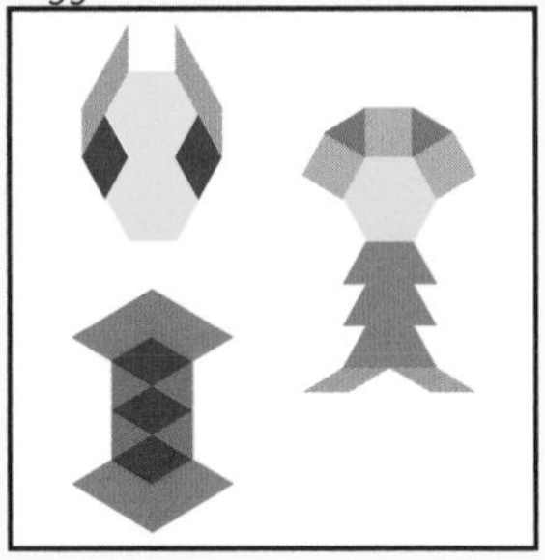

Page 69
Suggestion:

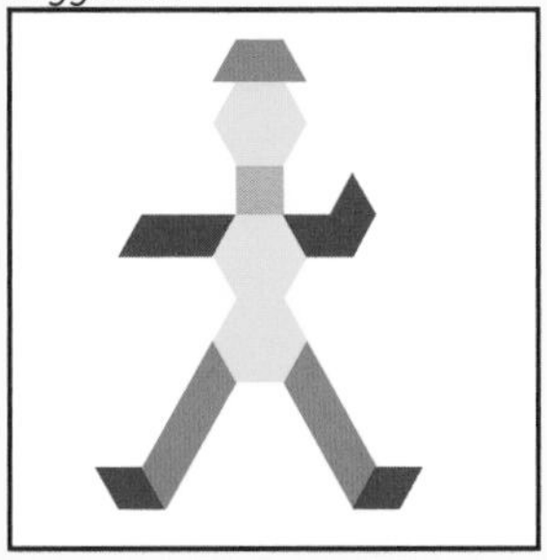

Page 70

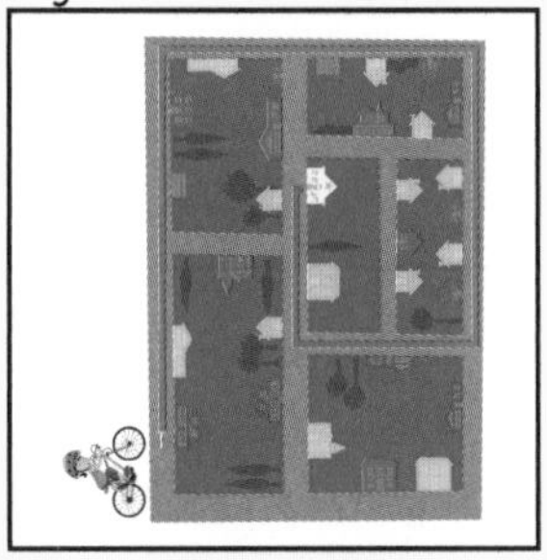

Page 71

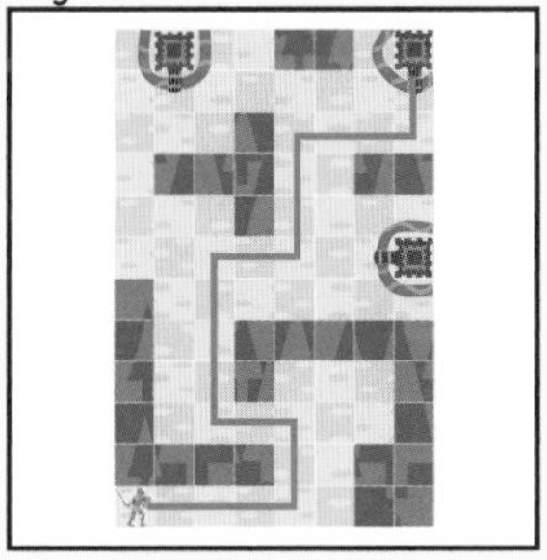

Pages 72–73

1. B7	2. E7
3. D5	4. A5
5. C3	6. D1
7. A2	8. E3
9. B1	

Page 74
Suggestion:

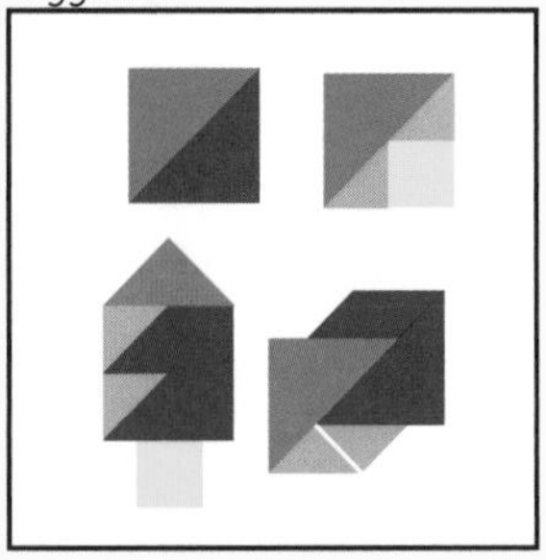

Page 75
Suggestion:

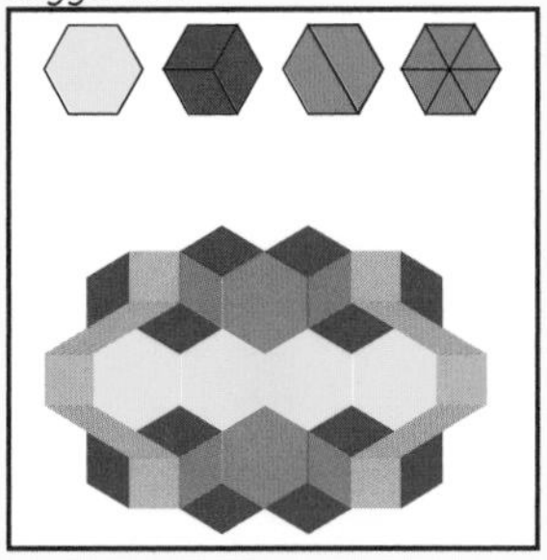

Page 76
Have someone check your answers.

Page 77
Have someone check your answers.

Page 78
1. nickel
2. quarter
3. penny
4. dime

Page 79

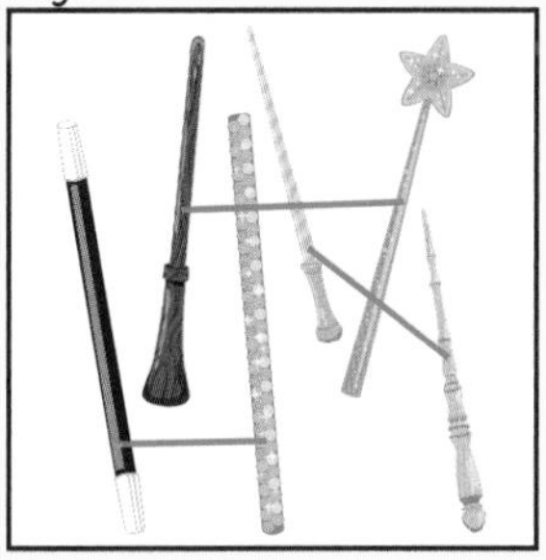

Page 80
An INCHWORM.

Page 81

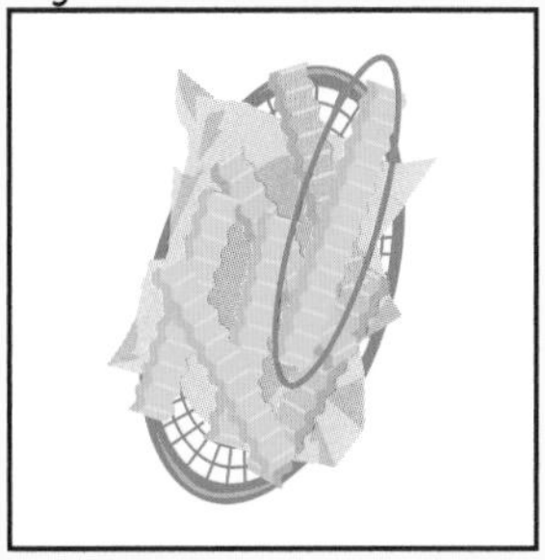

Page 82
SO LONG!

Page 83

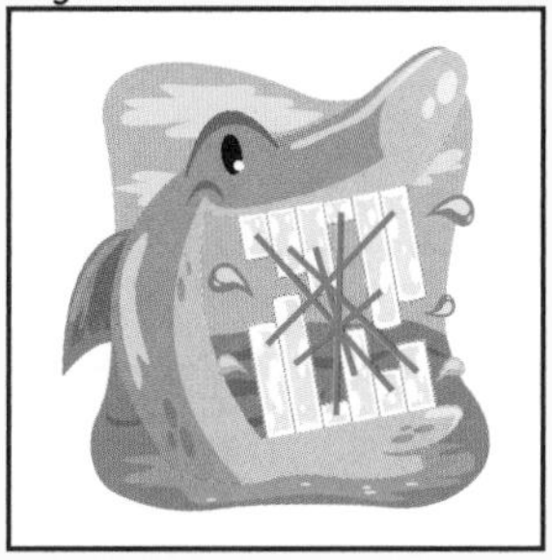

Page 84

1. 1	2. 3
3. 2	4. 5
5. 4	6. 6

Page 85
Each pair of lines is the same length.

Page 86

1. 4	2. 3
3. 2	4. 1
5. 7	6. 5
7. 6	8. 8

Page 87
Check:

1. 4	2. 5
3. 10	4. 7
5. 6	6. 9

Page 88

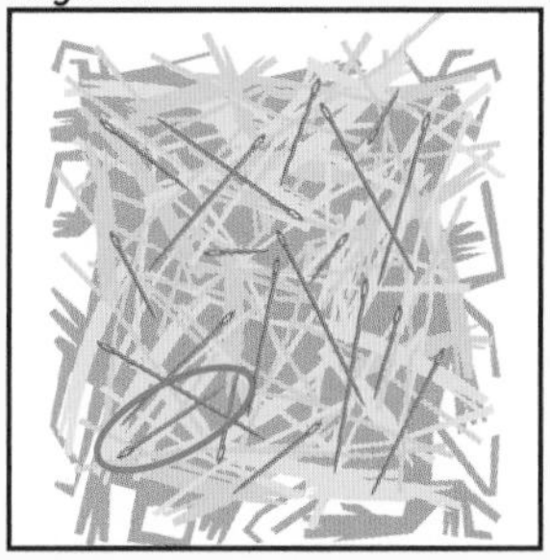

Page 89
Check:

1. 12	2. 9
3. 6	4. 8
5. 10	

Page 90

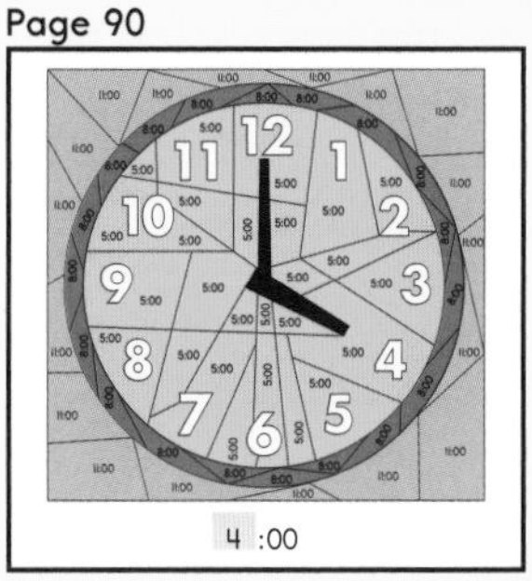

Answers

Page 91
Have someone check
your answers.

Page 93
Have someone check
your answers.

Page 94

11:30

Page 95
Have someone check
your answers.

Page 97

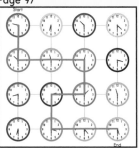

Page 98

Page 99

Page 100

1. 1¢	2. 25¢
3. 5¢	4. 11¢
5. 20¢	6. 15¢
7. 36¢	8. 17¢

IN A SNOW BANK!

Page 101
Have someone check
your answers.

Page 103

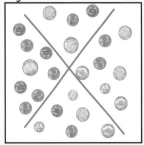

Page 104

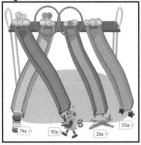

Page 105
Have someone check
your answers.

Page 107

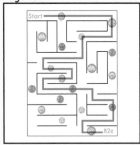

Page 108

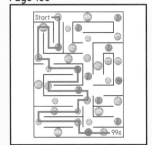

New Sylvan Learning Math Workbooks and Super Workbooks Help Kids Catch Up, Keep Up, and
Get Ahead!

From mastering the basics to having fun with newfound skills, Sylvan Learning Math Products can help students reach their goals, whether to do better on the next report card or get ahead for the following school year.

Workbooks use a systematic, age- and grade-appropriate approach that helps children find, restore, or strengthen their math skills.

Super Workbooks include three workbooks in one low-priced package—a great value!

Available Now
Basic Math Success Workbooks: Grades K-5

Kindergarten Basic Math Success
978-0-375-43032-9 • $12.99/$15.99 Can

First Grade Basic Math Success
978-0-375-43034-3 • $12.99/$15.99 Can

Second Grade Basic Math Success
978-0-375-43036-7 • $12.99/$15.99 Can

Third Grade Basic Math Success
978-0-375-43039-8 • $12.99/$15.99 Can

Fourth Grade Basic Math Success
978-0-375-43042-8 • $12.99/$15.99 Can

Fifth Grade Basic Math Success
978-0-375-43045-9 • $12.99/$15.99 Can

Available Now
Math Games & Puzzles Workbooks: Grades K-5

Kindergarten Math Games & Puzzles
978-0-375-43033-6 • $12.99/$15.99 Can.

First Grade Math Games & Puzzles
978-0-375-43035-0 • $12.99/$15.99 Can

Second Grade Math Games & Puzzles
978-0-375-43037-4 • $12.99/$15.99 Can

Third Grade Math Games & Puzzles
978-0-375-43040-4 • $12.99/$15.99 Can

Fourth Grade Math Games & Puzzles
978-0-375-43043-5 • $12.99/$15.99 Can

Fifth Grade Math Games & Puzzles
978-0-375-43046-6 • $12.99/$15.99 Can

On Sale May 2010
Math In Action Workbooks: Grades 2-5

Second Grade Math in Action
978-0-375-43038-1 • $12.99/$14.99 Can

Third Grade Math in Action
978-0-375-43041-1 • $12.99/$14.99 Can

Fourth Grade Math in Action
978-0-375-43044-2 • $12.99/$14.99 Can

Fifth Grade Math in Action
978-0-375-43047-3 • $12.99/$14.99 Can

On Sale July 2010
Math Success Super Workbooks: Grades 2-5

Second Grade Math Success
978-0-375-43050-3 • $18.99/$21.99 Can

Third Grade Math Success
978-0-375-43051-0 • $18.99/$21.99 Can

Fourth Grade Math Success
978-0-307-47920-4 • $18.99/$21.99 Can

Fifth Grade Math Success
978-0-307-47921-1 • $18.99/$21.99 Can

Also available: Language Arts Workbooks, Super Workbooks, and Learning Kits for Grades K-5

 All Sylvan Learning Workbooks include a coupon for a discount off a child's Skills Assessment at a Sylvan Learning Center®

Find Sylvan Learning Math and Language Arts Products at bookstores everywhere and online at:
sylvanlearningbookstore.com